This book belongs to

· ·

Draw a picture of yourself.

Go wild and color in!

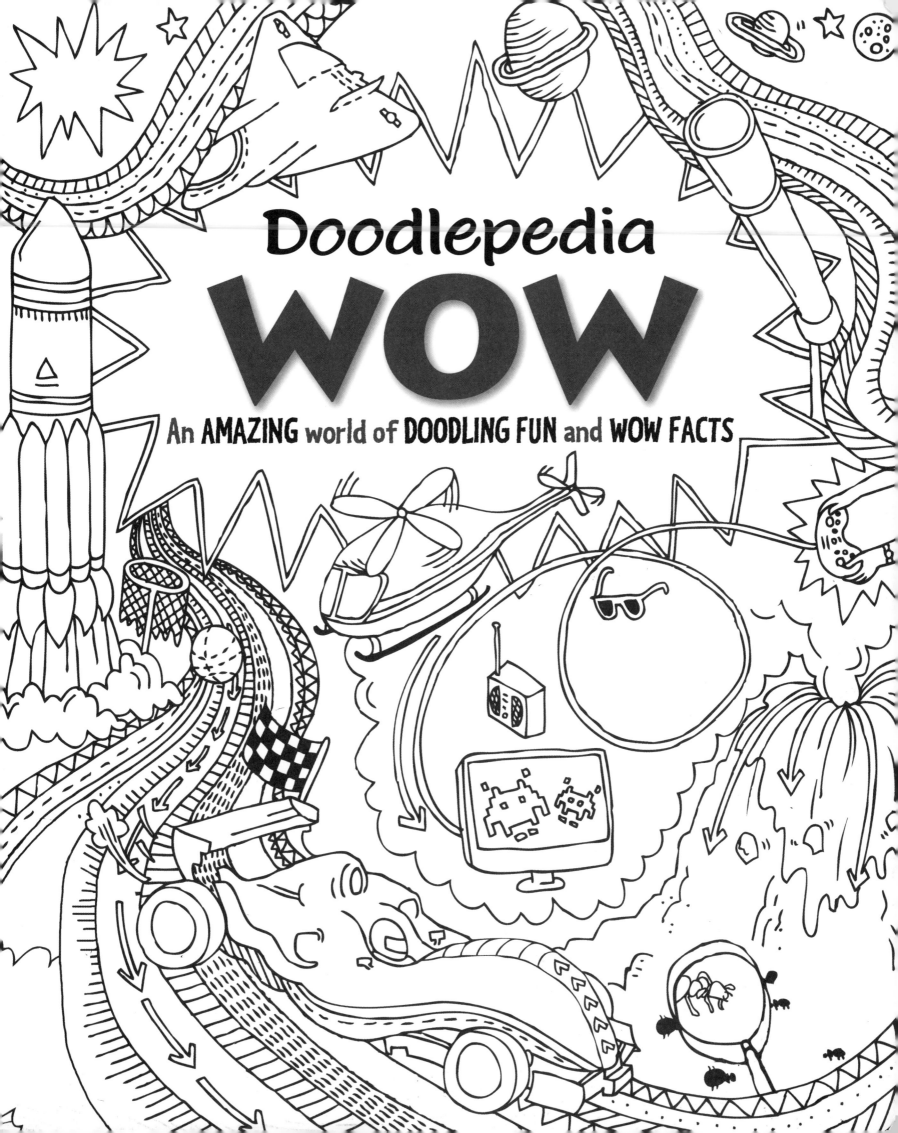

Doodlepedia
WOW

An AMAZING world of DOODLING FUN and WOW FACTS

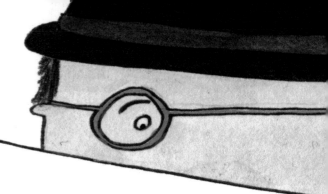

LONDON, NEW YORK, MELBOURNE, MUNICH, AND DELHI

Edited by Alexander Cox, Lee Wilson
Designed by Jess Bentall, Anna Formanek, Charlotte Johnson
Text by Alexander Cox, Wendy Horobin, Susan Maylan,
Ben Morgan, Lee Wilson
Fact checker Wendy Horobin
Illustrators Emma Atkinson, Holly Blackman,
Helen Dodsworth, Evannave, Nic Farrell,
Sean Gee, Rob Griffiths, Dan Woodger, Jay Wright
US Editor Margaret Parrish
Managing Editor Penny Smith
Managing Art Editor Marianne Markham
Art director Jane Bull
Category publisher Mary Ling
Producer (Preproduction) George Nimmo
Senior Producer (Preproduction) Tony Phipps
Senior Production Controller Seyhan Esen
Creative Technical Support Sonia Charbonnier

First published in the United States in 2012 by
DK Publishing, 375 Hudson Street, New York, New York 10014

Copyright© 2012 Dorling Kindersley Limited
12 13 14 15 16 10 9 8 7 6 5 4 3 2
002–185456—10/12

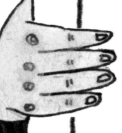

A catalog record for this book is available from the Library of Congress.
ISBN: 978-0-7566-9800-3
Printed and bound in China by Leo Paper Products Ltd.

All images © Dorling Kindersley
For further information see: www.dkimages.com

Discover more at www.dk.com

CREATE CRAZY CHEMICAL REACTIONS IN THE SCIENTIST'S LABORATORY.

FIND AND **COLOR** THE MISCHIEVOUS SPIDER MONKEYS.

Doodlepedia

An AMAZING world of DOODLING FUN and WOW FACTS

DESIGN YOUR OWN MASK.

DRAW MORE ROCKPOOL LIFE WAITING FOR HIGH TIDE.

GO DOODLING CRAZY IN THE EMPTY BOX.

DOODLEPEDIA is exactly what it says—a book of doodling! **COLOR**, **DESIGN**, and **DRAW** all over the pages and learn as you create. Find out about monster trucks, space, deep-sea fish, and lots more! Are you ready for oodles of doodling fun? Then turn the page and begin!

DISCOVER where these ants are going.

DRAW ants scurrying back to their home.

DESIGN an ultra-cool spy robot.

DRAW surfers and surfboards!

Surf's up!
Surfing is difficult and dangerous, but it's lots of fun! The trick is to hop onto the **surfboard** just before the wave **breaks** and then ride along the rolling wall of water. The best **surf waves** start life miles out to sea. Storms create **huge ripples** in the water that spread in all directions as waves. They may take days or even weeks to reach land. The waves break when they reach the beach because the shallow water makes the wave grow taller and taller—until it topples over.

Big-wave surfing involves waves more than 20 ft (6 m) high. Extreme surfers have ridden waves 70 ft (21 m) high—that's as tall as a seven-story building!

LEARN about poison frogs.

COLOR in my toxic friends.

COLOR IN THE BRIGHTLY PATTERNED **POISON DART FROGS.**

Toxic jumpers!
These rainforest-dwelling **amphibians** look colorful and friendly, but they are more **dangerous** than they seem. The bright patterns on the back of a poison dart frog tell predators not to eat it because it is **poisonous.** Rainforest tribes use the frogs's poison on the tips of their **blowpipe darts** when they hunt for food.

The **Golden Poison Dart** frog contains enough poison to **kill** 10 men.

Scientists believe the frogs get their poison from the insects they eat.

The race is on!

Car racing is fast and exciting. The cars that compete in Formula 1 can reach speeds of up to 225 mph (360 kph)! To make the cars safe, controllable, and fast, the engineers use the science of **aerodynamics**. A Formula 1 car is designed so the air that travels over and past it doesn't slow the car down too much. A Formula 1 car travels fast enough to take off like an airplane, so it also uses the pressure of the air flowing over it to keep it firmly on the track. This **downforce** allows the tires to grip the ground and gives the car more control.

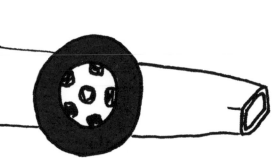

The **downforce** created by a Formula 1 car at its top speed is **strong enough** for it to be **driven upside down** along the roof of a tunnel.

DESIGN A WINNING, SUPERFAST **RACE CAR!**

Check your bags!

All luggage that is going on a plane has to be put through an airport **X-ray scanner**, which displays an image of what is inside each bag. The scanner operators are looking for **dangerous items**, such as weapons and other illegal things, but they must get to see some weird and wonderful things hidden in people's bags!

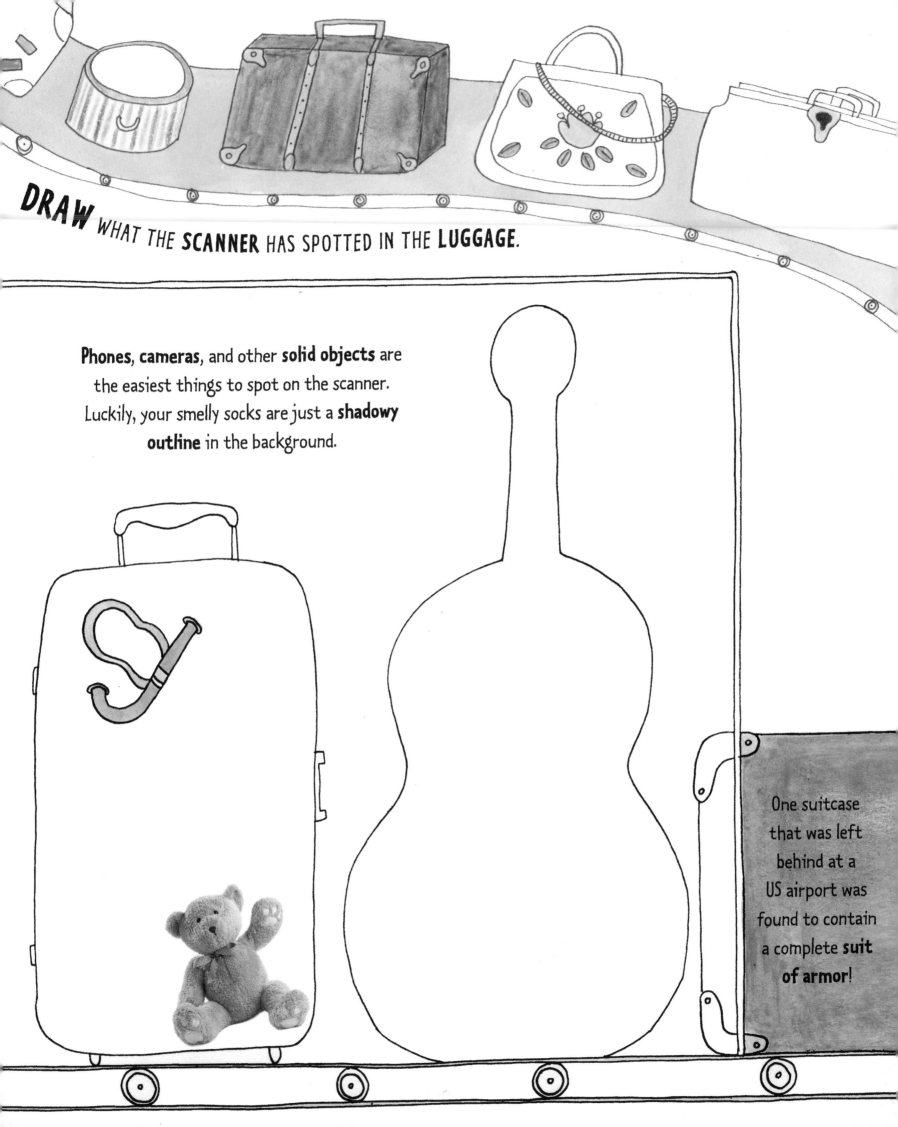

DRAW WHAT THE **SCANNER** HAS SPOTTED IN THE **LUGGAGE**.

Phones, cameras, and other **solid objects** are the easiest things to spot on the scanner. Luckily, your smelly socks are just a **shadowy outline** in the background.

One suitcase that was left behind at a US airport was found to contain a complete **suit of armor!**

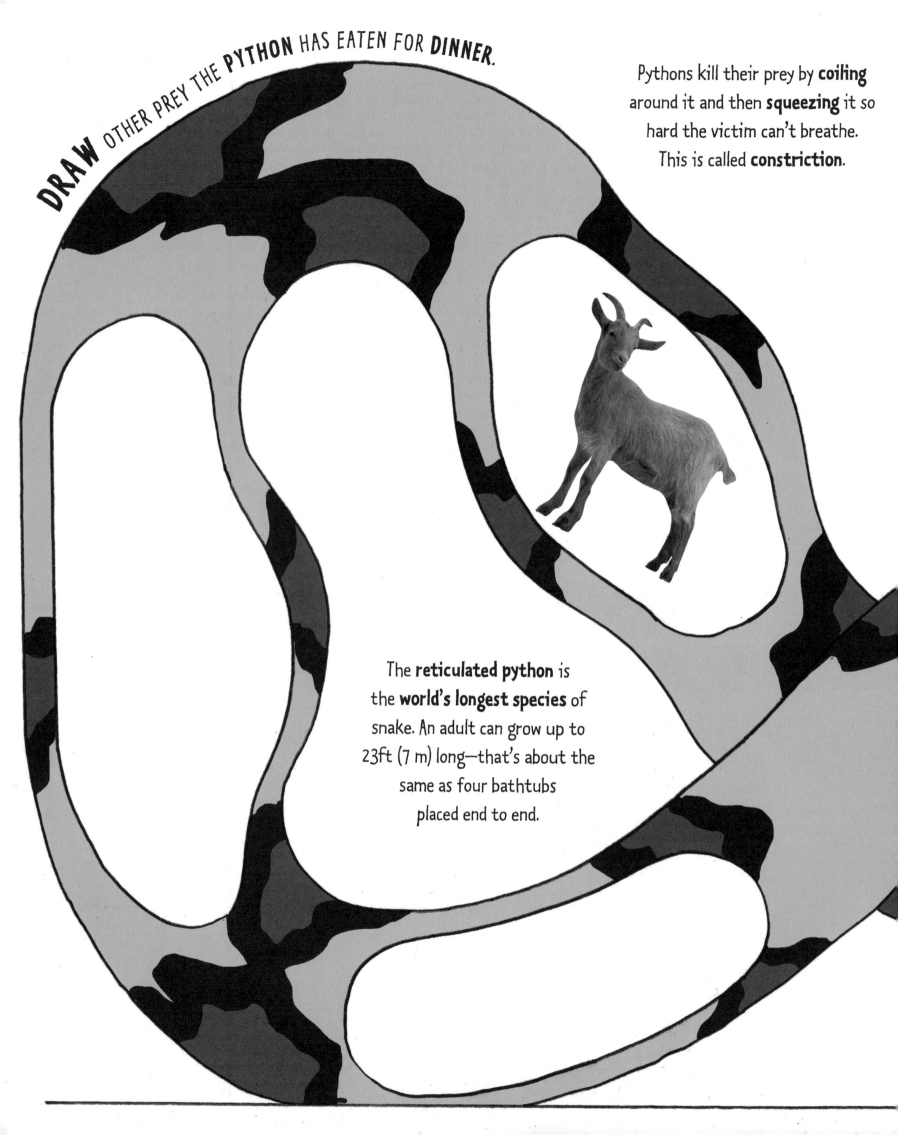

Pythons kill their prey by **coiling** around it and then **squeezing** it so hard the victim can't breathe. This is called **constriction**.

The **reticulated python** is the **world's longest species** of snake. An adult can grow up to 23ft (7 m) long—that's about the same as four bathtubs placed end to end.

Open wide!

Some large species of **python** really can eat a goat or a deer whole. But how does a snake swallow something that is bigger than its own mouth? The answer lies in its **jaws**, which are not hinged like ours but joined loosely by a **ligament**, like a piece of elastic. The ligament just keeps **stretching**, allowing the snake to open its jaws wider and wider until it has the whole prey in its mouth. Gulp!

Surf's up!

Surfing is difficult and dangerous, but it's lots of fun! The trick is to hop onto the **surfboard** just before the wave **breaks** and then ride along the rolling wall of water. The best **surf waves** start life miles out to sea. Storms create **huge ripples** in the water that spread in all directions as waves. They may take days or even weeks to reach land. The waves break when they reach the beach because the shallow water makes the wave grow taller and taller—until it topples over.

Big-wave surfing involves waves more than 20 ft (6 m) high. Extreme surfers have ridden waves 70 ft (21 m) high—that's as tall as a seven-story building!

Now wash your hands!

Viruses are a particularly nasty type of germ. They are very, very small—in fact, **millions** can fit on a pinhead only 2 mm wide! They can't survive for very long on their own, but once **inside the cells** of a living thing, such as a plant, animal, or person, they can grow and **reproduce** very fast, making people feel very sick.

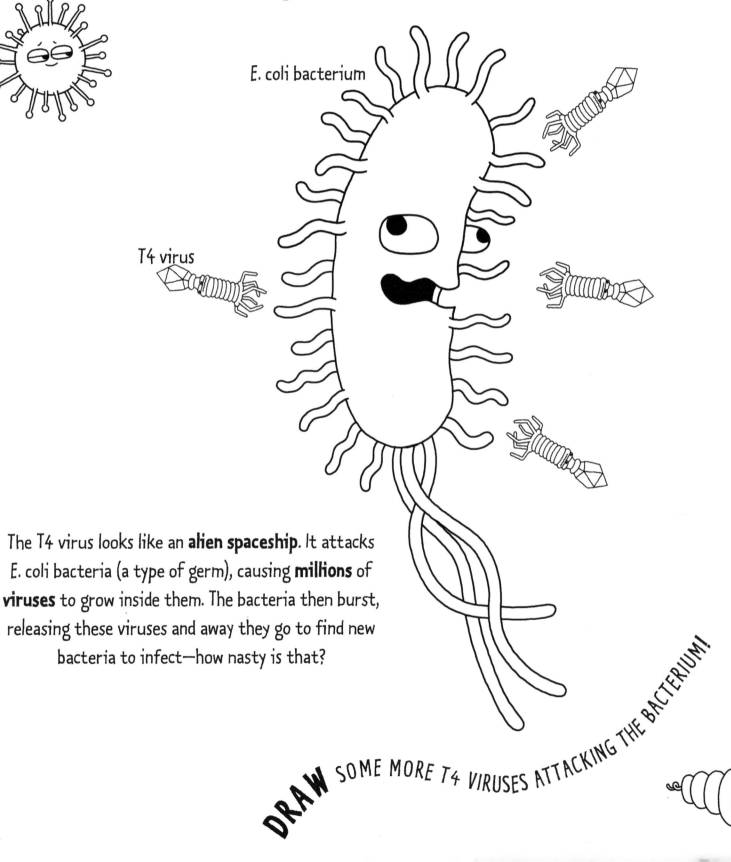

E. coli bacterium

T4 virus

The T4 virus looks like an **alien spaceship**. It attacks E. coli bacteria (a type of germ), causing **millions** of **viruses** to grow inside them. The bacteria then burst, releasing these viruses and away they go to find new bacteria to infect—how nasty is that?

DRAW SOME MORE T4 VIRUSES ATTACKING THE BACTERIUM!

DRAW AND COLOR SOME MORE VIRUSES.

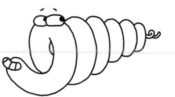

Most **viruses** are between
5–300 nanometers (nm) long.
Considering that a nanometer is
1,000,000,000th of a meter,
that is pretty small!

The **Coup de Monde** is given the winners of the **FIFA World Cup**.

FIFA WORLD CUP

This **spiral** trophy is given to the winner of the **Giro d'Italia** bicycle stage race.

Giro d'Italia

It's a winner!

Nothing beats coming **first** in a sport and winning a **trophy**! In ancient times, winners at sporting events were often awarded a **silver goblet**. The tradition continues to this day, with **giant gold and silver trophies** given to **winning athletes and teams** in many major tournaments. To crown their moment of **glory**, winners may hold their trophy aloft and revel in the crowd's **cheers and applause**.

DESIGN SOME SHINY MEDALS.

DESIGN YOUR OWN WINNER'S TROPHY.

Medals are awarded at the **Olympic Games** to **athletes** who finish first, second, or third in their event final.

We need a hero!

HELP!!! The evil villain, cunningly disguised as a burglar, is making off with all the loot. Who can stop him? **Comic strips** like this one have been **entertaining** people since they were first published in 19th-century **newspapers**. Some of the most-loved characters are **superheroes**, such as Batman, Superman, and the Incredible Hulk.

Oh, no! A dastardly robber has taken a valuable painting...

HELP! WE NEED A SUPERHERO!

... but your superhero is here to help! Let's go get that cunning crook!

DRAW YOUR OWN SUPERHERO AND **FINISH** THE STORY.

"Hmm. Here's a clue that will lead me to the stolen painting..."

"... This is a great time to test out my new superhero gadget."

"Got you at last! Stop struggling, you scoundrel!." POW! CRASH! CRUNCH!

"It's off to the jail cell for you! Handcuff him!"

THE END!

COLOR THE MISCHIEVOUS SWINGING MONKEYS.

Baby spider monkeys travel everywhere by keeping a **tight grip** on their mothers, especially when Mom is **hanging upside down.**

Spider monkeys don't have any **thumbs**, but still have a powerful grip.

Hanging around!

Spider monkeys spend all day **hanging** around in the rainforests of South America. They are incredibly **agile**, swinging from branch to branch in search of their favorite foods, which include fruits, seeds, birds' eggs, and insects. They get their name from their **long, spidery arms and legs**. Their **tails** are longer than their bodies and they can use them like an extra limb. This allows them to use their hands and feet for feeding while keeping a **firm grip** on a branch using only their tails.

Mask of art!

African tribal masks can look strange, scary, and fantastic. They have been a part of tribal life in Africa for thousands of years and are still used today in **dances, rituals, and ceremonies**. The **skill** of making the tribal masks is handed down from father to son and the **mask-maker** is given a special role in the tribe. The masks are usually based on human faces, but aren't very realistic.

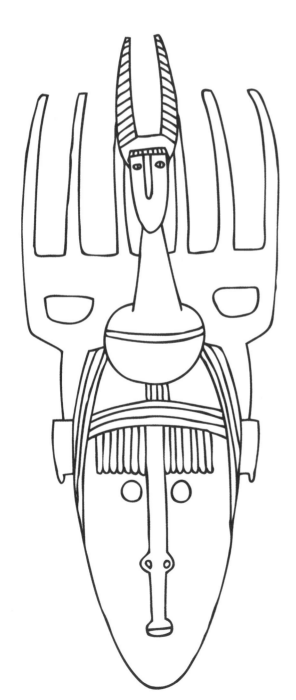

Some masks are **sacred** and are thought to possess **magical powers**.

Tribal mask makers would use materials that were close to hand, like **wood, stone, and ivory** (animal tusks). The masks were painted using **local dyes** from **plants and soil**.

DESIGN YOUR OWN TRIBAL MASK.

Down under in Australia!

When the first European **explorers** set out to map **Australia**, they had no idea what hideous **hazards** lay ahead. The middle part of the country, called the **Outback**, turned out to be a vast, **desertlike plain**, with **baking temperatures** and very **little water**. Many explorers died there from thirst, hunger, and disease. The wildlife was not always friendly either—the Outback contains some of the worlds' most **poisonous snakes** and **spiders**.

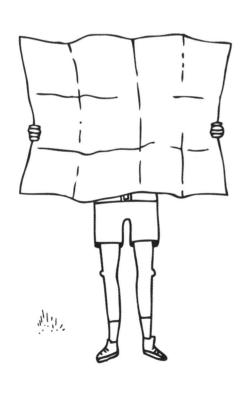

DRAW THE EXPLORERS' CAMPSITE AND **ADD** MORE HAIRY CAMELS AND SLITHERING SNAKES.

The explorer **Charles Sturt** thought there was an inland sea in the **Outback** so he took a boat with him!

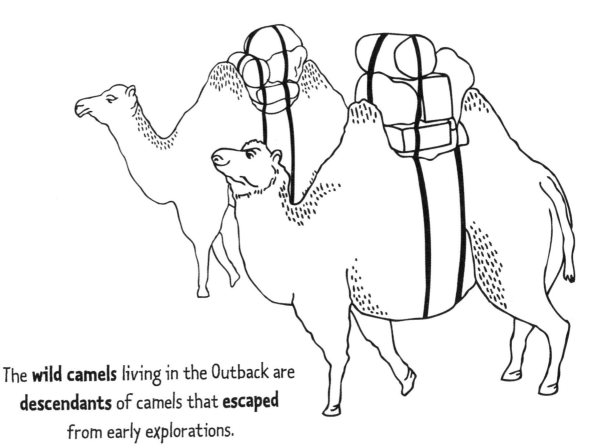

The **wild camels** living in the Outback are **descendants** of camels that **escaped** from early explorations.

Goal!

Soccer is the most popular sport on the planet, with an **incredible 3.5 billion fans worldwide**—that's more than half the world's population! The rules of the modern game were drawn up in Cambridge, England, in 1863, but soccer was **invented more than 2,000 years ago in China**. It caught on in England about 800 years ago, before being **banned for 300 years** after games got too violent. Today, soccer is played in **every country** in the world.

DRAW MORE PLAYERS AND MAKE A WHOLE TEAM.

Whistles were introduced to soccer in 1878, but the **yellow and red cards** were not used until the 1970 World Cup in Mexico.

The **first-ever World Cup** took place in Uruguay in 1930, and **80,000 people watched** the match.

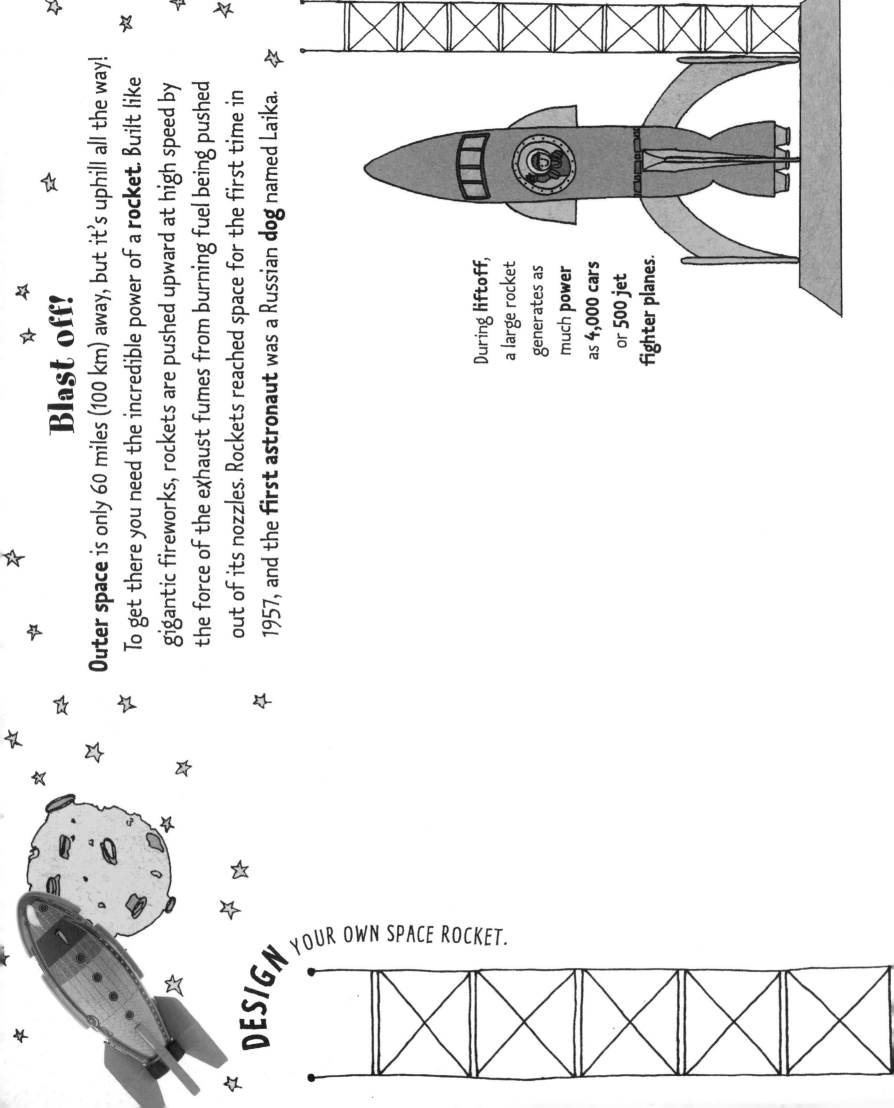

Blast off!

Outer space is only 60 miles (100 km) away, but it's uphill all the way!

To get there you need the incredible power of a **rocket**. Built like gigantic fireworks, rockets are pushed upward at high speed by the force of the exhaust fumes from burning fuel being pushed out of its nozzles. Rockets reached space for the first time in 1957, and the **first astronaut** was a Russian **dog** named Laika.

During **liftoff**, a large rocket generates as much **power** as **4,000 cars** or **500 jet** fighter planes.

DESIGN YOUR OWN SPACE ROCKET.

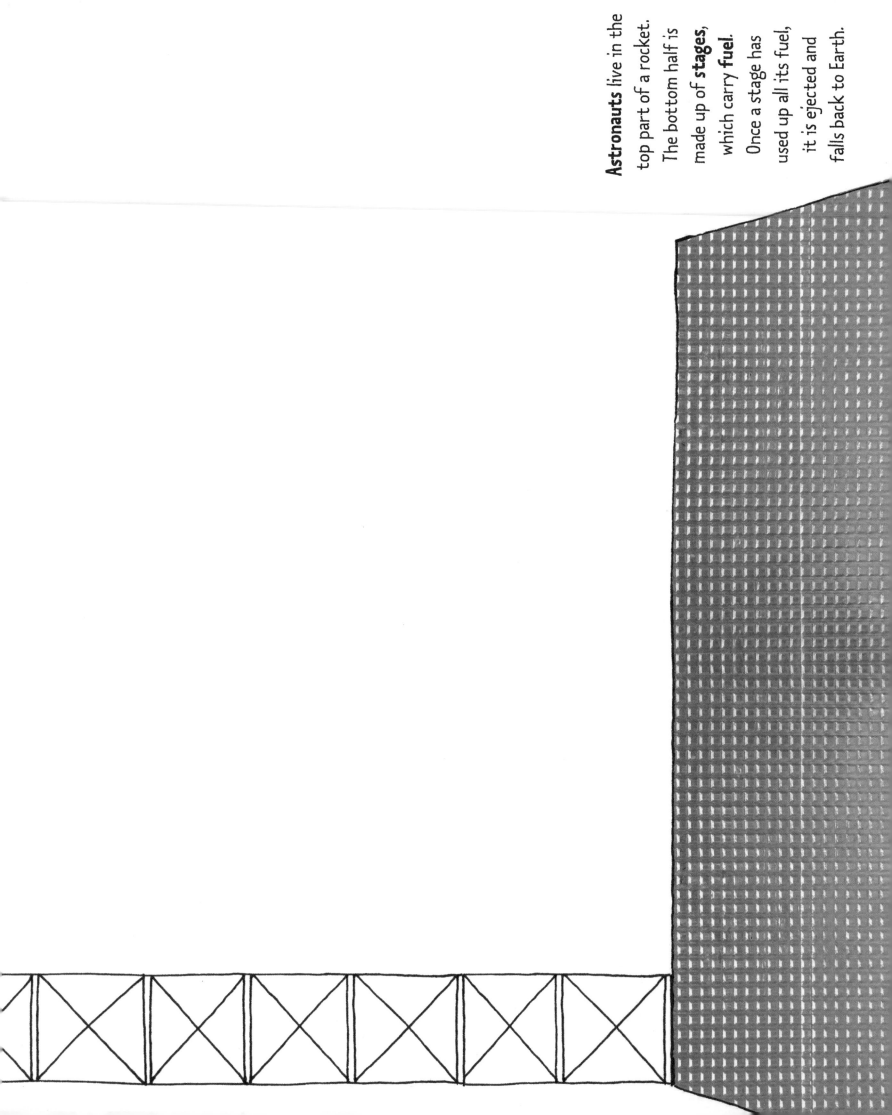

Astronauts live in the top part of a rocket. The bottom half is made up of **stages,** which carry **fuel.** Once a stage has used up all its fuel, it is ejected and falls back to Earth.

Toxic jumpers!

These rainforest-dwelling **amphibians** look colorful and friendly, but they are more **dangerous** than they seem. The bright patterns on the back of a poison dart frog tell predators not to eat it because it is **poisonous**. Rainforest tribes use the frogs's poison on the tips of their **blowpipe darts** when they hunt for food.

One, two, three... jump!

Imagine sitting by an open door of a plane 2.5 miles (4 km) up and being told to jump—scary! For the first 60 seconds you're on your own, free-falling through the sky at speeds of 120 to 180 mph (190 to 290 kph). At 0.5 mile (760 m) above the ground it's time to open your parachute. You'll land in six to seven minutes, so be prepared!

Some say **skydiving** feels like **flying** rather than falling. If you are a beginner, you can **"tandem skydive,"** strapped to an instructor.

Experienced skydivers take part in brief, **death-defying** aerial displays. In 2008, **400 skydivers** joined up for 4 seconds to form a **spiral shape**—a free-fall formation **world record!**

DRAW AND **COLOR** SOME MORE SKYDIVERS.

It's cold out there!

Life can get **very chilly** in the Arctic regions around the **North Pole**, especially in the winter. The **animals** that live there have special adaptations to help them live with the cold. Most have a **fur coat** or lots of feathers to help them **keep warm**. A type of **Arctic fish** has a special protein in its blood that stops it from **freezing solid**. Some animals spend many months asleep in **dens and burrows** when food gets scarce. Others go on long journeys **to escape** the bad weather and search for food.

AAHHHHA bah h h h hh

DRAW SOME MORE ANIMALS ON THE ICE.

Arctic foxes and Arctic hares **turn from brown to white** in winter to help them **hide** from predators.

WHAT IS THE POLAR BEAR CHASING?

Insects galore

Some **900,000** different kinds of living insect have been identified and named, but scientists believe that there are still many more out there that have yet to be discovered. Some say there could be more than **30 million** different kinds of insect in total!

It's been estimated that there are 10 quintillion individual insects alive at any one time — that's **a 10 with 18 zeros** after it!

Approximately **80%** of all the animal species in the world are insects!

DRAW SOME MORE INSECTS AND CREATE A **BUG FEST**!

Earth's gravity still has an effect on people in space—just not as much. If a **ladder connected** the Earth and a **spacecraft in orbit**, and you climbed up it, you would **weigh 11% less** at the top! So if you weigh 60 lb (27 kg), you'd only weigh about 53 lb (24 kg) at the top of the ladder.

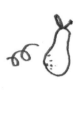

Floating in space

Did you know that **astronauts are not really weightless**? Instead, they are **just constantly falling** toward Earth, together with the spacecraft and everything inside it. So **why don't they fall out of the sky**? Well, the Earth's surface is curved. As the spacecraft and its contents fall to Earth, they are also **traveling extremely fast "sideways."** The Earth's surface curves away from them as fast as they are falling so they end up **orbiting** the Earth and never reach the surface.

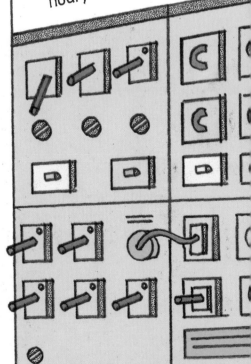

To remain in orbit, the **International Space Station** must travel about 17,500 miles per hour (28,000 km per hour)—now that's fast!

DRAW THE ASTRONAUTS FLOATING AROUND THEIR **SPACE STATION**.

To stop the colossal building from collapsing into the sea, **giant concrete pillars** beneath it descend 80 ft (25 m) below sea level.

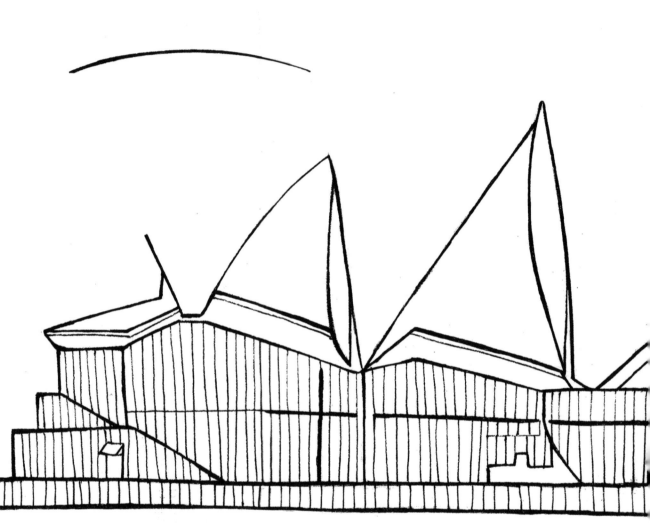

Welcome to Australia!

Sydney Opera House is Australia's most famous building and a masterpiece of **modern architecture**. Surrounded by the glittering waters of beautiful **Sydney Harbour**, it resembles a **flotilla of boats**, their white sails filled by the wind. The "sails" consist of 10 vast concrete **shells** covered with **gleaming white and cream tiles**. Inside are **seven halls**, the largest of which contains one of the **world's largest pipe organs**, with more than 10,000 pipes.

There are more than **1 million** glossy white and cream tiles on the roof of the Sydney Opera House.

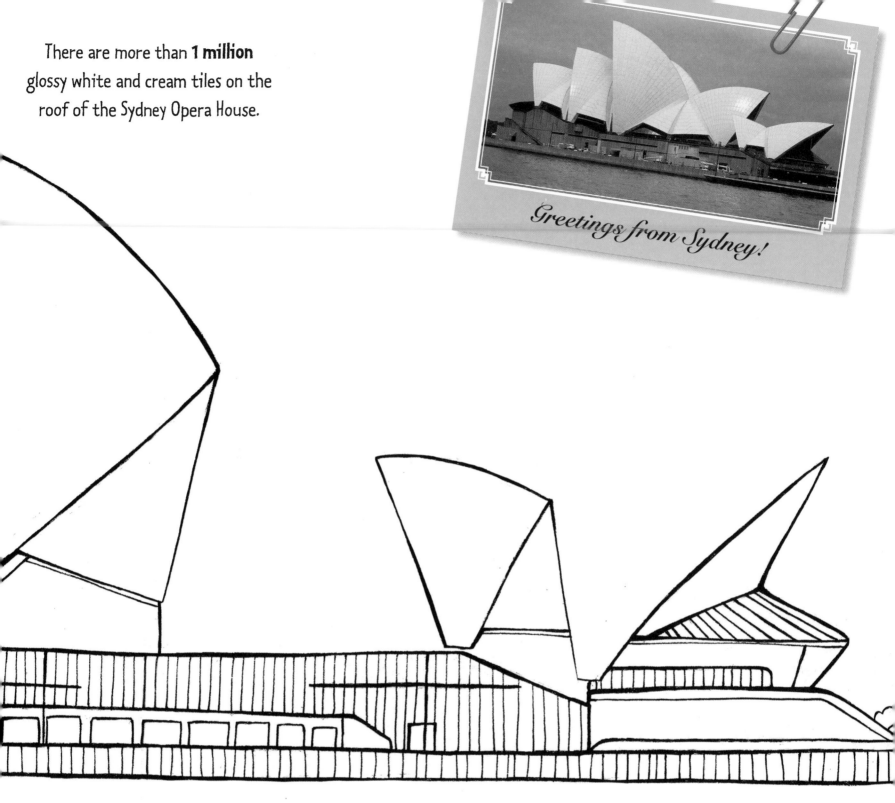

Greetings from Sydney!

DRAW MORE **BOATS** IN THE **HARBOR**.

DRAW WHAT'S LIVING IN THE ROCKPOOL.

The **Goby Rock fish** has a **suction cup** on its underside, which it uses to **cling** to rocks so it doesn't get **washed away** with the tide.

It's a hard life!

One minute it's **low tide** and the sun is beating down and evaporating water from the **rockpool** shallows, making them saltier than usual; the next minute, it's **high tide**, huge waves are crashing down onto the pools, and the water temperature is dropping. These are the **daily living conditions** that any creature or plant living in a rockpool has to cope with if it is to **survive**.

DRAW SOME MORE SKIERS AND SNOWBOARDERS—WHO WILL BE THE FIRST TO MAKE A JUMP?

Nerves of steel!

Extreme skiing and snowboarding take a lot of **nerve and skill**. An **extreme skier** can reach speeds between 125 and 155 mph (200 and 250 kph), and **extreme snowboarders** have been known to go as fast as 125 mph (200 kph)! Traveling this fast, they have to have their wits about them so they can **dodge obstacles** such as rocks, trees, and crevasses (tricky), **avoid avalanches** (almost impossible!), and be able to complete **amazing jumps** successfully!

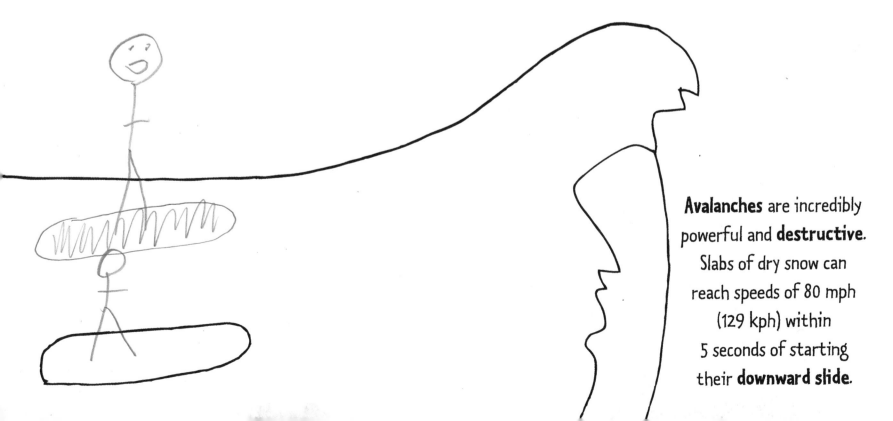

Avalanches are incredibly powerful and **destructive**. Slabs of dry snow can reach speeds of 80 mph (129 kph) within 5 seconds of starting their **downward slide**.

DESCRIBE OR **DRAW** A **TYPICAL DAY** IN YOUR NOTEBOOK.

BURIED BY

.........Marco.................

Spacecraft have even taken time capsules into space for **future space travelers** to find. Voyager 1 and 2 have a gold-plated, copper phonograph record on board, containing pictures and sounds of **life on Earth**. It will take around **40,000 years** before the spacecraft reach another planetary system!

Future treasures!

Have you ever thought about making a **time capsule** and leaving it for people to discover many years from now? Time capsules commonly contain **photos, diaries, and objects** so that future generations can have a "**snapshot**" of what life was like in the past. A time capsule in Nebraska has a **white pyramid** above ground to mark where it is buried. It has around **5,000 items** inside it—including **two cars!**

DRAW WHAT YOU WOULD STORE IN YOUR **TIME CAPSULE.**

Follow that termite!

A **termite mound** is like an iceberg—only a little sticks up and the rest, including **tunnels**, is hidden from view. Made entirely from **termite poop, spit**, and **mud**, the mound can reach 26 ft (8 m) tall and 120 tons (110 metric tons) in weight. Hidden in the maze of tunnels are as many as a **million termite workers** and their **king** and **queen**.

The top part of a termite mound works like a **chimney**, letting warm air escape. This keeps the **temperature** underground **just right**.

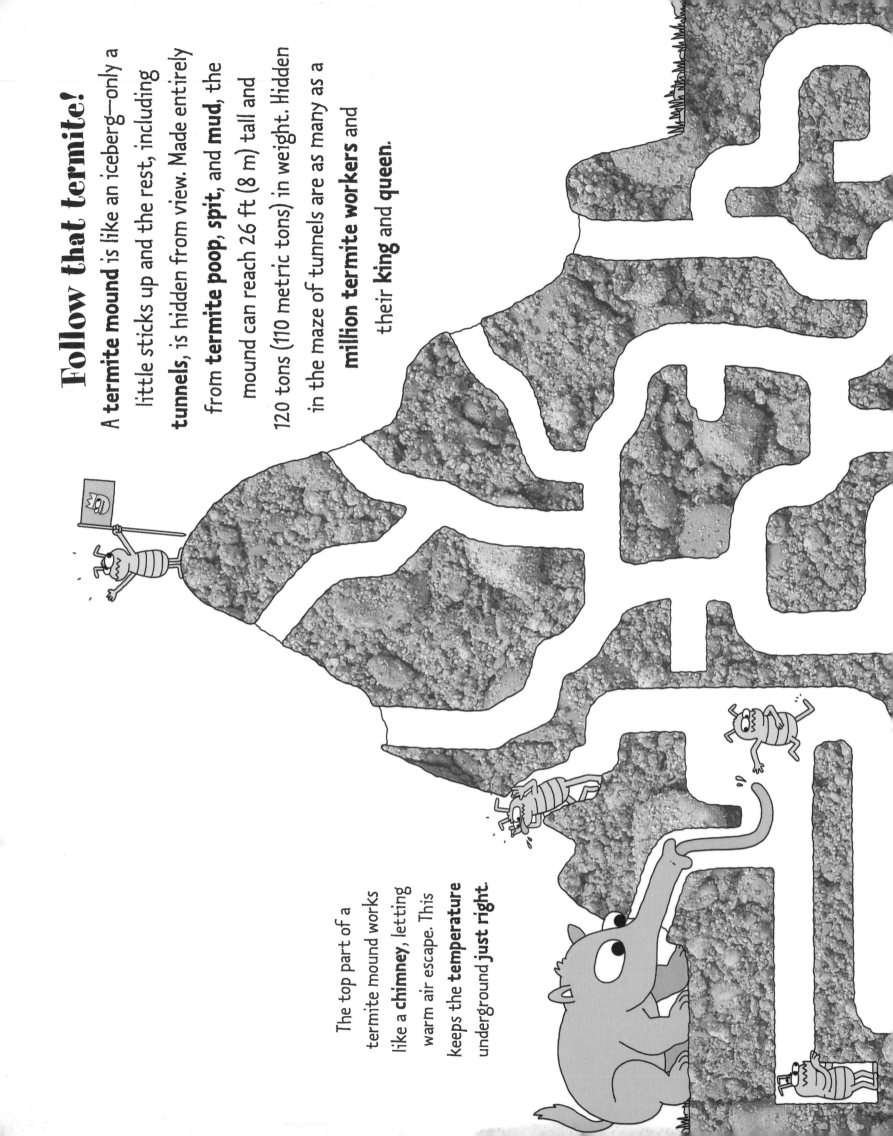

FIND THE WAY TO THE **BOTTOM** OF THE **MOUND** AND BACK OUT OF THE **TOP**.

Sometimes the mere whiff of a **smell** can make you recall a long-forgotten memory.

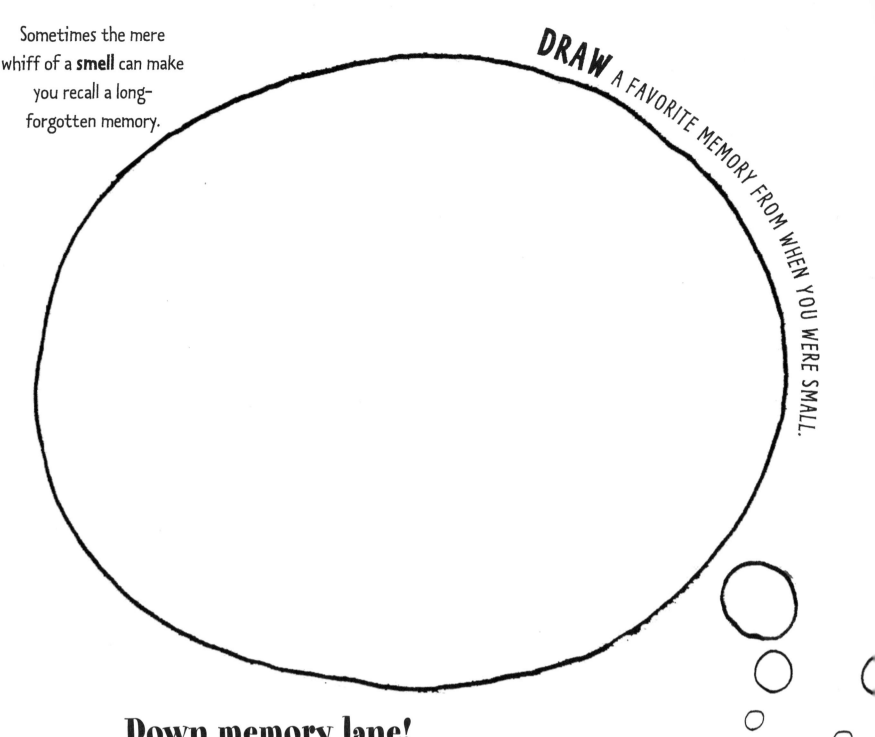

DRAW A FAVORITE MEMORY FROM WHEN YOU WERE SMALL.

Down memory lane!

How much do you remember from your first day at school? We can recall **memories** from the past thanks to our **short-term memory**, which briefly stores all the things we see, hear, smell, touch, and taste. Some of these memories then move to **long-term** storage, allowing us to remember them months or years later. There isn't just one place in our **brains** where our memories are kept, but a part of the brain, called the **hippocampus**, plays a vital role in turning short-term memories into long-term ones.

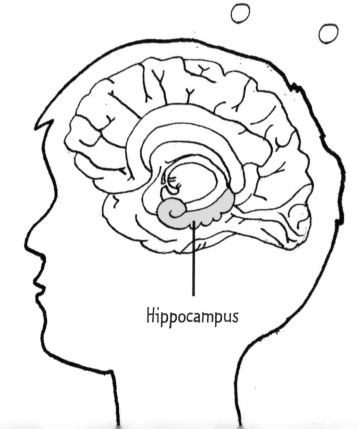

Hippocampus

DRAW YOUR
EARLIEST MEMORY.

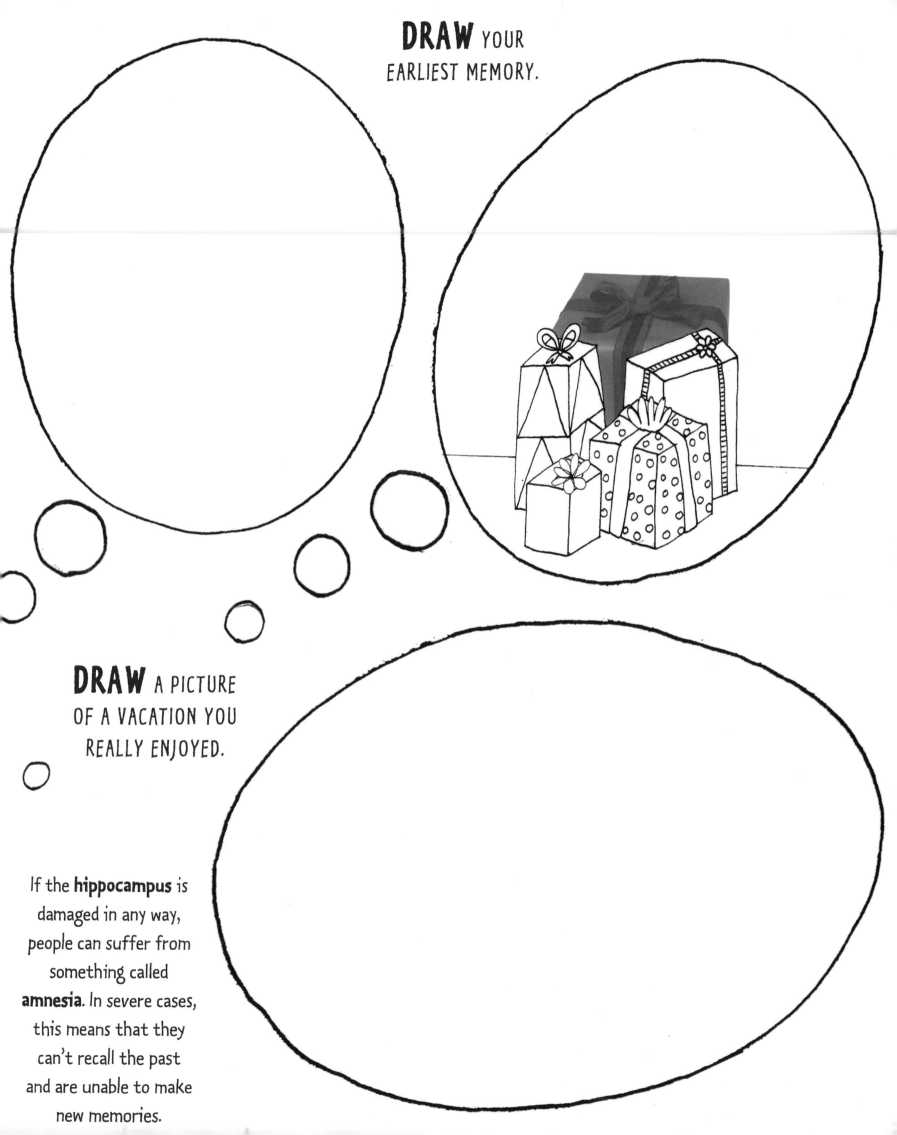

DRAW A PICTURE
OF A VACATION YOU
REALLY ENJOYED.

If the **hippocampus** is
damaged in any way,
people can suffer from
something called
amnesia. In severe cases,
this means that they
can't recall the past
and are unable to make
new memories.

Gaming world!

Things have certainly changed a lot since the first **video games** were **invented** in the 1970s. Today, the games industry employs thousands of people worldwide and makes more than twice as much money as the movie industry in the US alone. It takes a

Games can be based on **any subject**—sports, cartoons, racing, action adventures, and much, much more.

DESIGN YOUR OWN CONSOLE GAME.

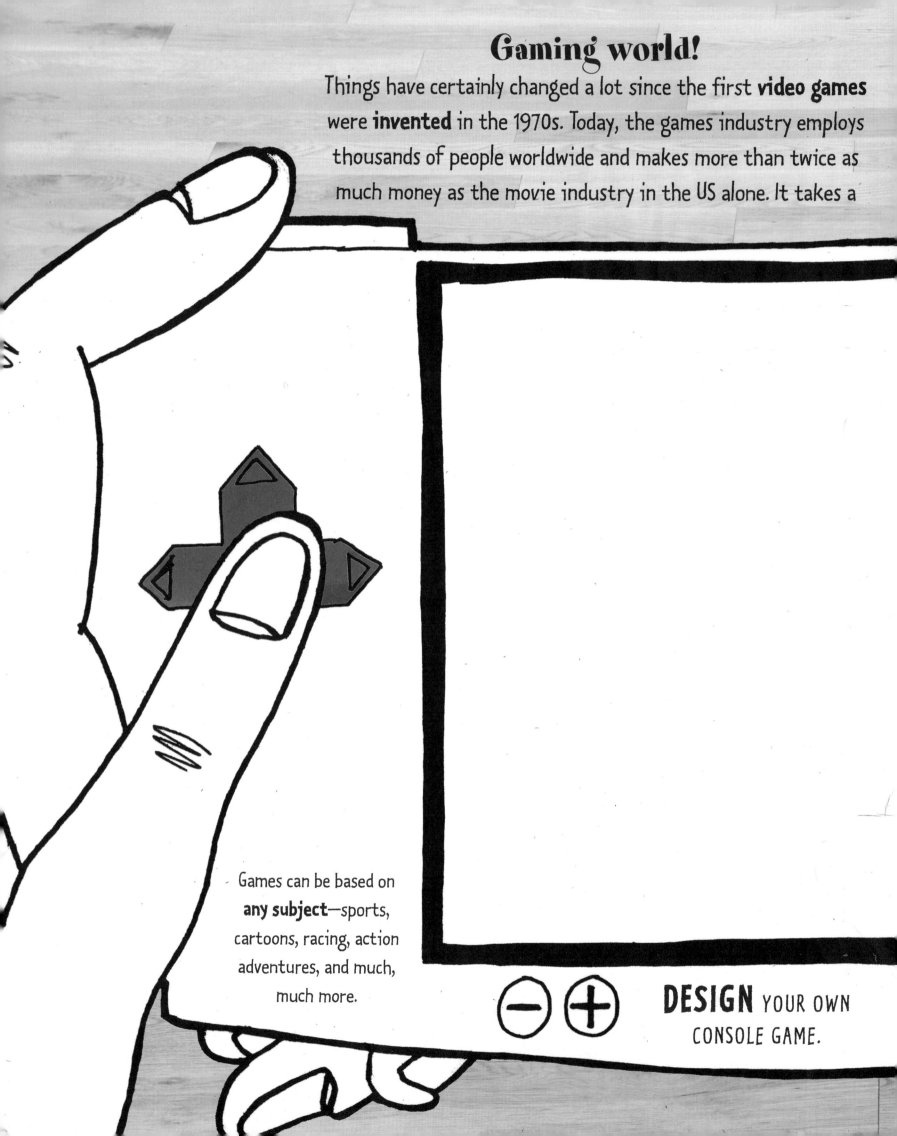

team of up to 50 people to create a **video game**, including programmers, graphic designers, artists, sound designers, musicians, and game testers. Other teams design the **consoles** themselves. So if you love playing video games, this could be the career for you!

The **first handheld electronic game**, *Auto Race*, was launched in 1976. The graphics were very basic—the player's car was just a bright blip on a tiny screen.

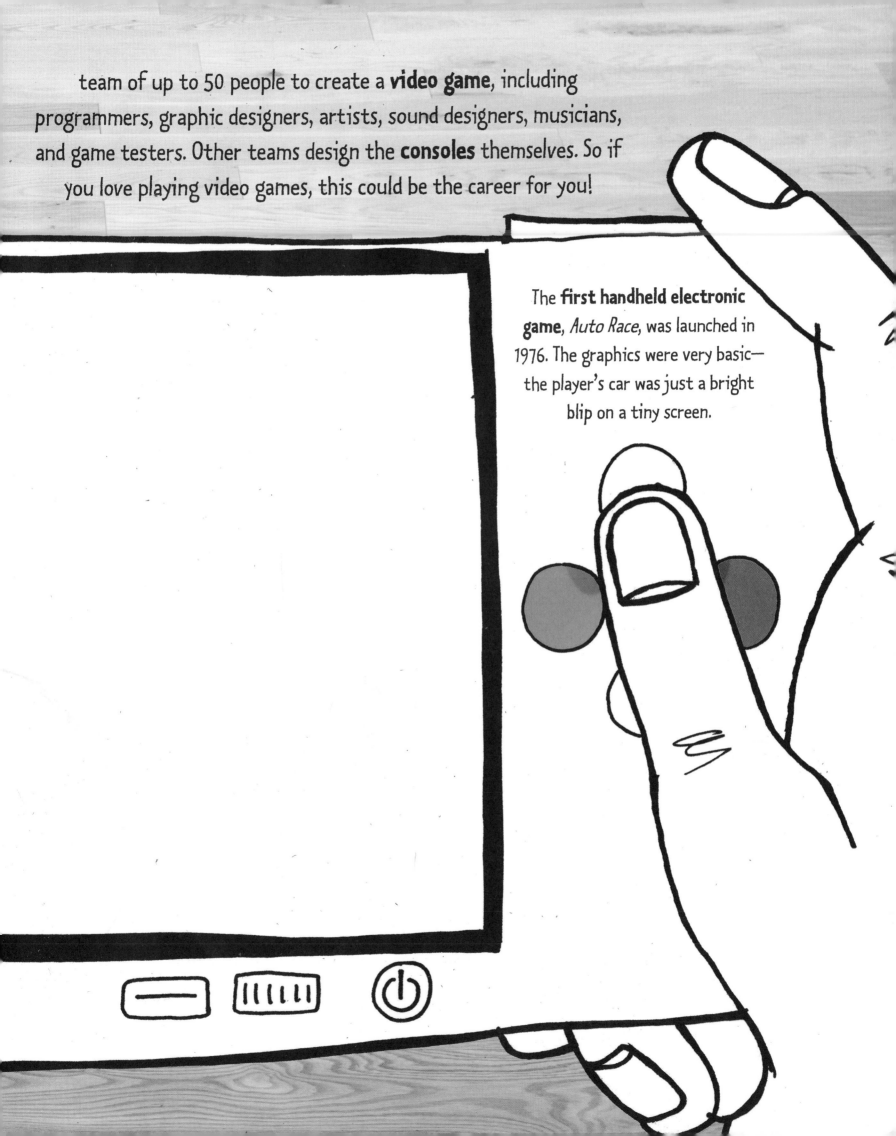

Mount Everest is 29,035 ft (8,848 m) tall, and it is **still growing**! Every year it gets a few millimeters higher due to movements of the **Earth's crust**.

On top of the world!

Intrepid **climbers** from all over the world travel to **Nepal** for the ultimate challenge—conquering **Mount Everest**, the **world's tallest mountain**. It's a dangerous climb, so dangerous that the area above 26,000 ft (8,000 m) is known as the **"death zone."** Climbers have to battle with **high winds**, **subzero temperatures**, and **low oxygen levels**. But it's all worth it for the magic moment when they reach the **summit** and stand on the very top of the world!

DRAW MORE FEARLESS CLIMBERS.

Many climbers who get into difficulties on Everest are **rescued by helicopter**. In 2005, one helicopter set a record for the highest ever landing by touching down on the summit!

The **stripes** are not just fur deep—if you shaved a tiger, the **skin** would be striped underneath, too!

DRAW THE TIGER'S STRIPES.

A tiger's **terrifying**, loud **roar** can be heard as far as 2 miles (3 kilometers) away.

DRAW SOME MORE TIGERS PROWLING THROUGH THE GRASS.

Prowling in the shadows!

Normally an animal's camouflage helps it to hide from predators, but a tiger's **striped skin** helps it to hide from its **prey**. The lines break up the outline of its body, helping the tiger blend into shadows created by the long grass. This means it can **creep up on its victim** without being spotted. A tiger's stripes are as unique as fingerprints are to people; no two tigers have the same pattern.

DRAW YOUR OWN **AMAZING** EXPERIMENTS AND EXPLOSIONS.

Our **bodies** are full of chemical reactions. There are more than 100 trillion cells in the human body and **each cell** produces **thousands** of **chemical reactions**. That adds up to quite a lot!

Bubble, fizz, bang!

Everything in the world, in fact, everything in the universe, is made up of stuff, or as the scientists like to call it, **matter**. When **energy**, such as heat, light, or electricity is **added to matter**, changes called chemical reactions can take place—occasionally they can be very **explosive**! Scientists experiment with chemical reactions in **laboratories**, but they happen all around you and inside you, too!

Rotting food is a chemical reaction! **Bacteria** (a germ) and fungi cause irreversible changes in food. They also create quite a **stink**!

Extremely dry!

The **Atacama Desert** in Chile, South America, is a very thirsty place. Situated high in the **Andes Mountains**, some weather stations there have never recorded a **single drop of rain**. The mountains are the reason for this. They are so high that rainclouds coming in from the Pacific Ocean are forced to drop their load of water on the coastal side of the mountains in order to rise over the tops. By the time the clouds have reached the Atacama on the other side, there is practically **no water** left.

Space scientists test their **space robots** in the Atacama Desert, since the **landscape is similar to that of Mars.**

DESIGN YOUR OWN SPACE ROBOT.

ADD SOME MORE **SHAGGY** LLAMAS.

Incredibly wet!

There are several contenders for the title of **wettest inhabited place** on Earth. It all depends on how you measure it. One of them is **Lloró** in Colombia. This town receives 44 ft (13.3 m) of rain spread throughout the year. Another contender is **Mawsynram** in India. This gets 39 ft (11.8 m), although most of this falls during the short **monsoon season**.

Cloudbursts can drop 4 in (10 cm) of rain in an hour.

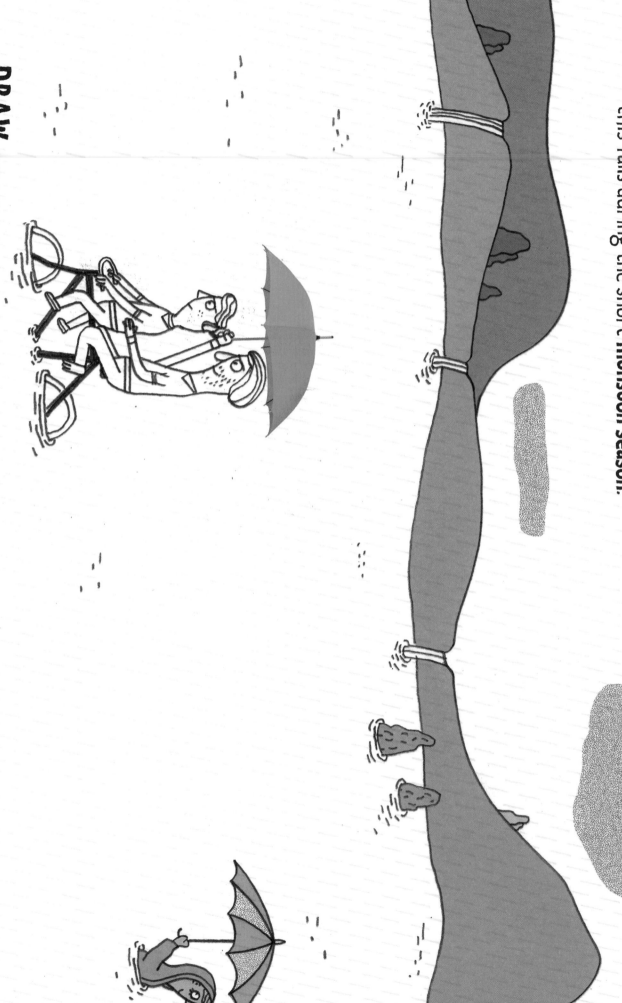

DRAW HOW YOU WOULD GET ACROSS THE FLOOD.

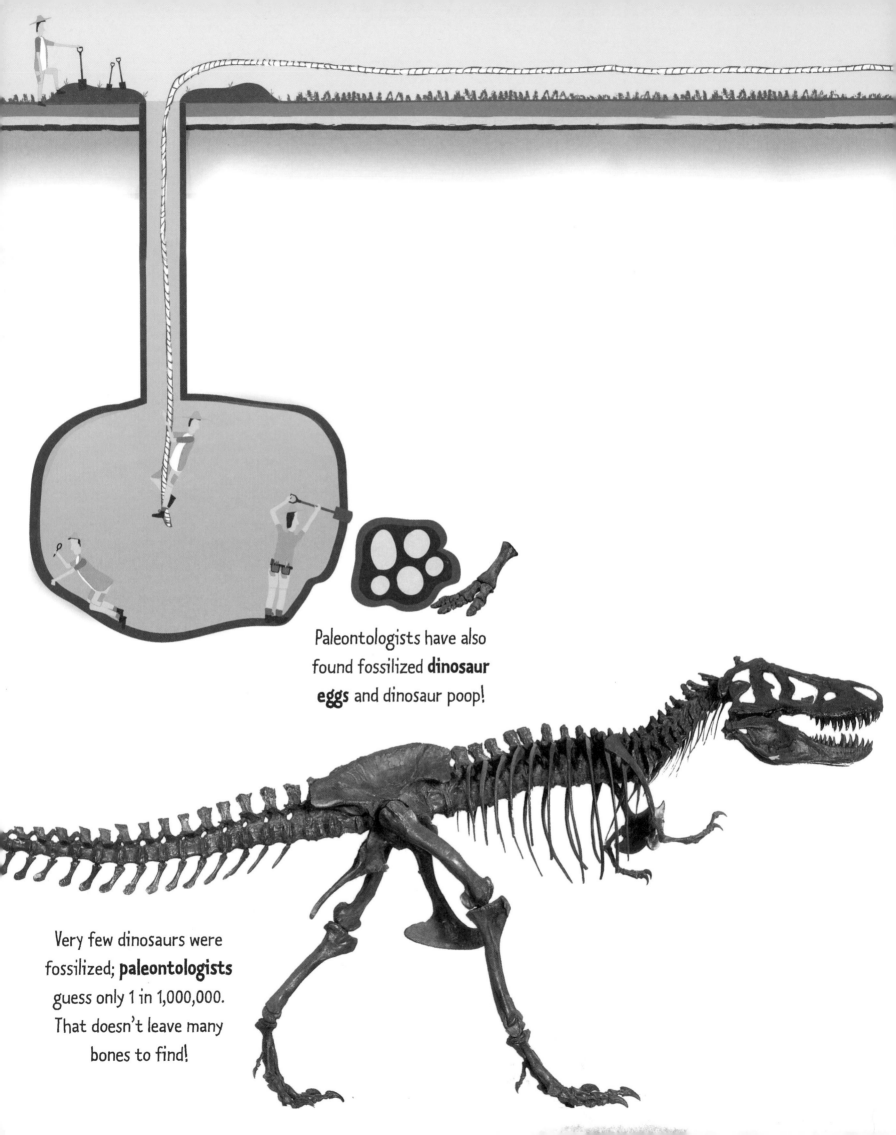

Paleontologists have also found fossilized **dinosaur eggs** and dinosaur poop!

Very few dinosaurs were fossilized; **paleontologists** guess only 1 in 1,000,000. That doesn't leave many bones to find!

Buried bones

Everything we have learned about dinosaurs comes from their **fossilized remains**. Fossils need certain conditions to form. When a dead dinosaur gets covered in sand or mud, its bones are **preserved** and over millions of years the sand and mud turn to rock. The **bones** of the dead dinosaur **absorb** minerals and harden into fossils— ready for dino-seekers (paleontologists) to find them.

DRAW SOME FOSSILIZED BONES FOR THE PALEONTOLOGISTS TO DISCOVER.

Viking attack!

If you had lived a thousand years ago, this is something you would not have wanted to see—a boatful of scary **Vikings**! These fierce warriors from **Scandinavia** terrorized people all over Europe, **raiding** their towns and villages, **stealing** anything valuable they could grab, and leaving a trail of d**eath and destruction** behind them.

A Viking warrior wore a **metal helmet** and carried a **shield**. He was armed with a **sword**, **ax**, or **spear** and was not afraid to use it!

The Vikings crossed the sea in wooden ships, called **longboats**, powered by oars and a sail and decorated with a dragon's head.

DRAW MORE FEARSOME **FIGHTERS** TO COMPLETE THE **VIKING ARMY**.

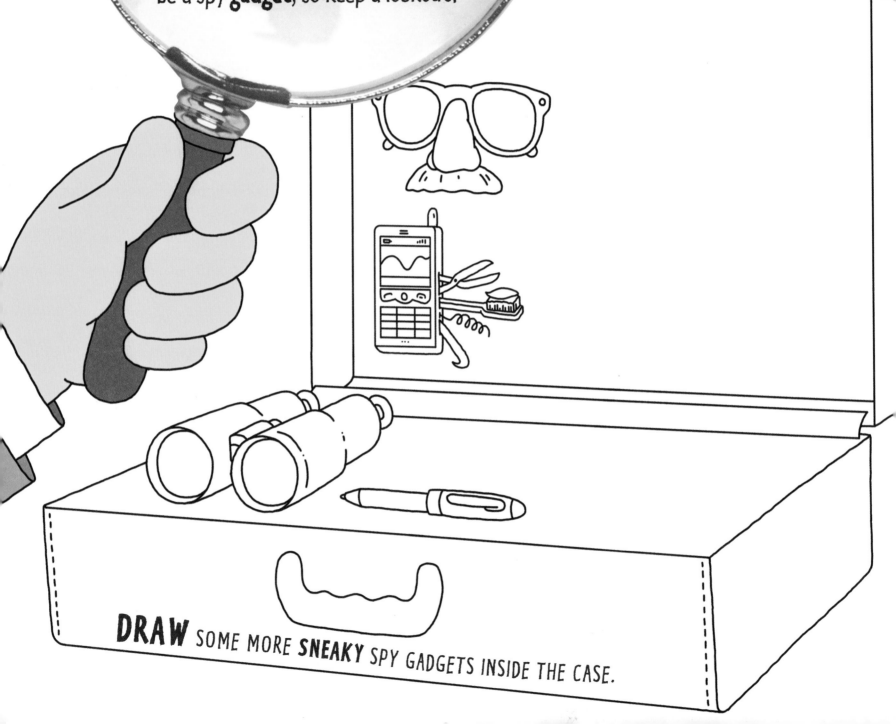

Supercool gadgets!

Have you ever wanted to be a **spy**? You'll need some cool gadgets to help you. How about sunglasses with a **hidden camera**, night-vision **goggles** for spying after dark, a voice-activated pen to records conversations, or a **roving robot** that can do the spying for you. What may appear to be a normal everyday object, may in fact be a spy **gadget**, so keep a lookout!

A spy is a person employed to **collect secret information**, known as **"intelligence,"** about another country's government, military, or industries.

DRAW SOME MORE **SNEAKY** SPY GADGETS INSIDE THE CASE.

DESIGN AN ALL-SEEING, ALL-HEARING, COOL SPY ROBOT.

The largest bats have a wingspan
of more than 5 ft (1.5 m).

DRAW MORE **BATS** FLYING AT NIGHT.

Most bats sleep upside down during the day inside caves, hollow trees, and even houses!

A bit batty

Bats are **flying mammals**. Most bats eat insects, although some eat fruit, blood, and even other bats! Bats aren't blind—their eyesight is nearly as good as humans—but because they hunt at night they need a little extra help, and use **echolocation** to find prey and to stop them from bumping into things. A bat makes high frequency sounds (adult humans can't hear them), which bounce off prey. The bat then listens for the echo, which allows it to locate its supper.

They are two main types of
curved mirror, **concave** ones that
curve in and **convex** that bulge
out. To know which is which,
just remember caves go in,
and so do concave mirrors!

Bendy reflections!

Have you ever been in a **hall of mirrors** at an amusement park or circus?
The mirrors are designed to create **strange and bizarre reflections**.
Some mirrors make you really tall, while others make you really short.
How do the mirrors work? The mirrors **aren't flat** like the ones you have
at home. Instead, they are **warped and curved** so they **reflect** light rays
back at **strange angles**, creating the fun and weird reflections.

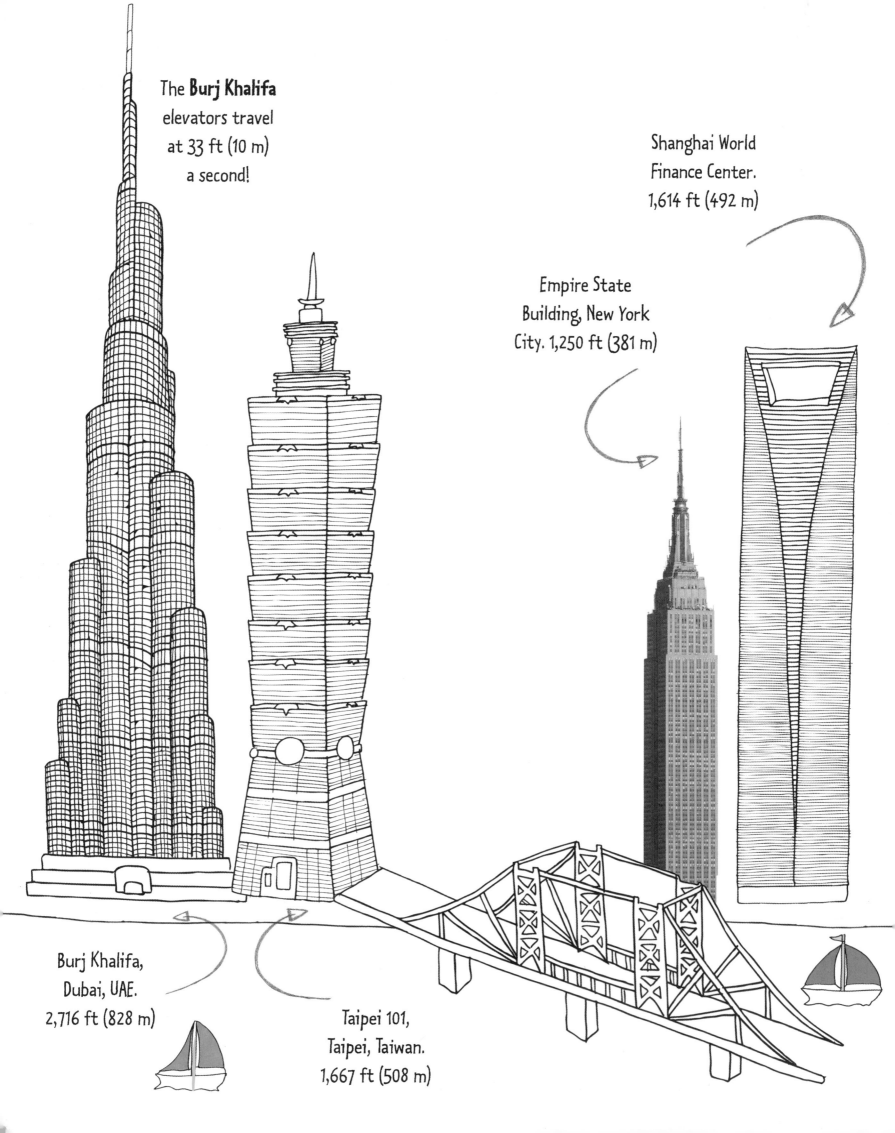

The **Burj Khalifa** elevators travel at 33 ft (10 m) a second!

Shanghai World Finance Center. 1,614 ft (492 m)

Empire State Building, New York City. 1,250 ft (381 m)

Burj Khalifa, Dubai, UAE. 2,716 ft (828 m)

Taipei 101, Taipei, Taiwan. 1,667 ft (508 m)

Higher and higher and higher...

There have always been **tall buildings**—just think of the **Egyptian pyramids**. However, until the mid-19th century, a building's height was limited by the **number of stairs** people were willing to climb and how much **weight** brick walls could support. Two inventions changed all that—the **elevator** (no more stairs—whoopee!) and the use of a **steel frame** to **support the building**. Since then, buildings have rocketed **skyward**!

The Shard, London, United Kingdom. 1,016 ft (310 m)

Petronas Towers, Kuala Lumpur, Malaysia. 1,482 ft (452 m)

DESIGN YOUR OWN **SKYSCRAPERS**—*THE SKY'S THE LIMIT!*

Incredibly cold!

Imagine a place where pen ink **freezes** and metal sticks to skin. Welcome to **Oymyakon**, the **coldest inhabited village** on Earth! Situated in **Siberia, Russia**, the temperature here has been known to go as low as −96.16°F (−71.2°C). Winter lasts for **nine months** of the year and children are not allowed outside to play for more than **20 minutes** at a time because the **extreme cold** could damage their lungs.

Strangely enough, Oymyakon is named after a nearby **hot spring**!

DRAW YOURSELF AND YOUR FRIENDS PLAYING OUTSIDE—WRAP UP WARMLY!

Extremely hot!

Dallol in Ethiopia currently holds the record for the world's **highest average temperature**. Most days the thermometer reaches 94°F (34°C), but it can go as high as 148°F (64°C) in the summer. Only a few people live here—it's miles from anywhere, there are no real roads, and abandoned cars that have broken down are still awaiting recovery! The only reliable transportation is a camel.

The landscape is brightly colored red, yellow, and white from the mineral salts that evaporate from **volcanic springs** underground.

COLOR THE LANDSCAPE IN REDS, YELLOWS, AND WHITE.

DRAW SOME REALIBLE CAMELS.

It took the **crew** of a steam train nearly **three hours** to generate enough steam to get the train moving.

DRAW THE MISSING WAGON—WHAT'S INSIDE THEM ALL?

All aboard!

The first trains were called **steam trains** because they were **powered** by steam and belched out great clouds of **steam** and **smoke**. The engine car at the front contained a huge **coal fire** that was used to boil water and turn it into steam, which then traveled through pipes and pushed **pistons** (rods) that turned the wheels around. Steam engines generated fantastic power—enough to pull a long row of heavy cars.

DESIGN YOUR OWN TRAIN.

Terrors from the deep!

Life on Earth most likely started in **the oceans**. There are **millions of species** of animal that live in the oceans, some we haven't yet discovered because the oceans are so **vast and very, very deep**. Some of the fish that live in the oceans are very **strange and unique**.

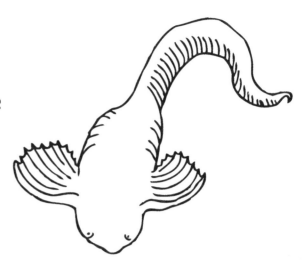

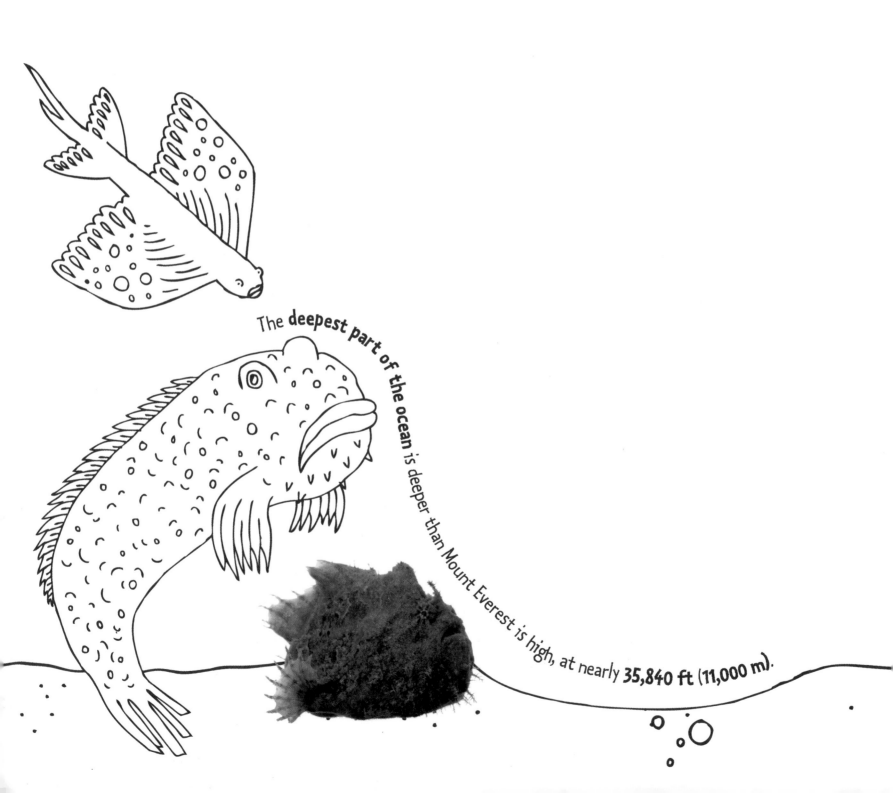

The **deepest part of the ocean** is deeper than Mount Everest is high, at nearly **35,840 ft (11,000 m)**.

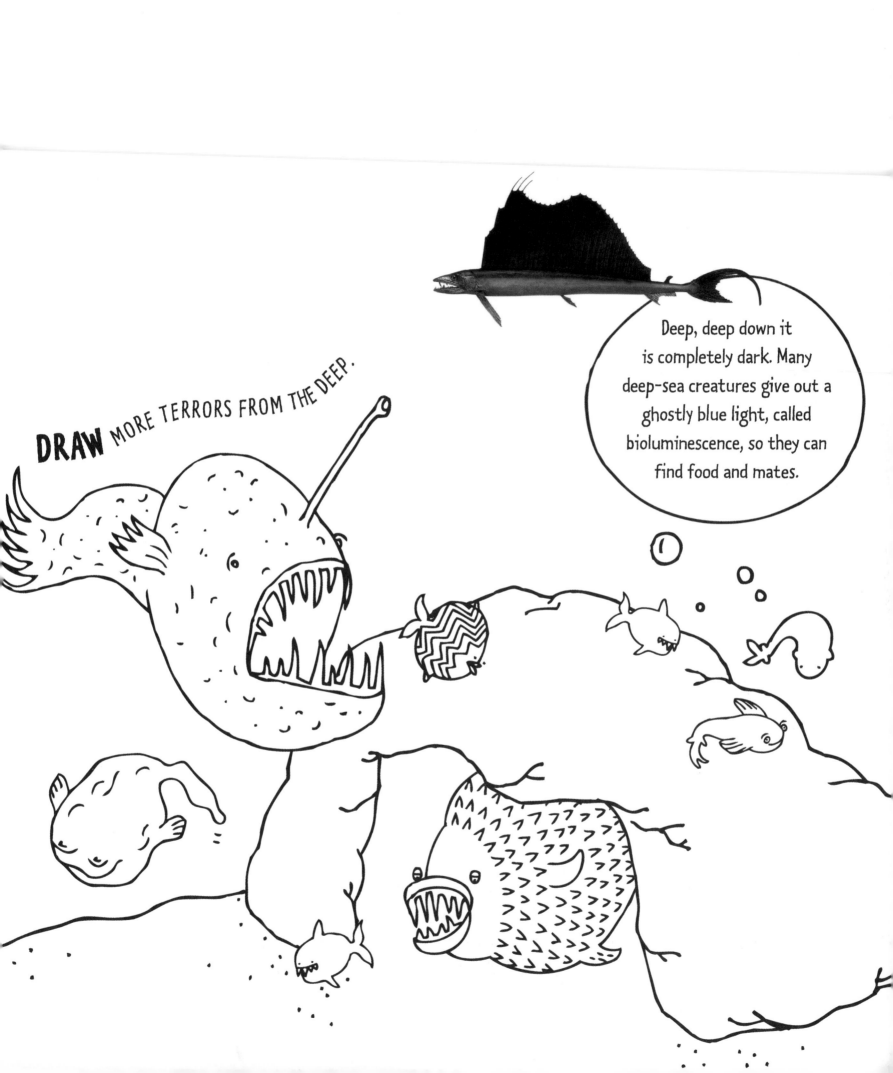

DRAW MORE TERRORS FROM THE DEEP.

Deep, deep down it is completely dark. Many deep-sea creatures give out a ghostly blue light, called bioluminescence, so they can find food and mates.

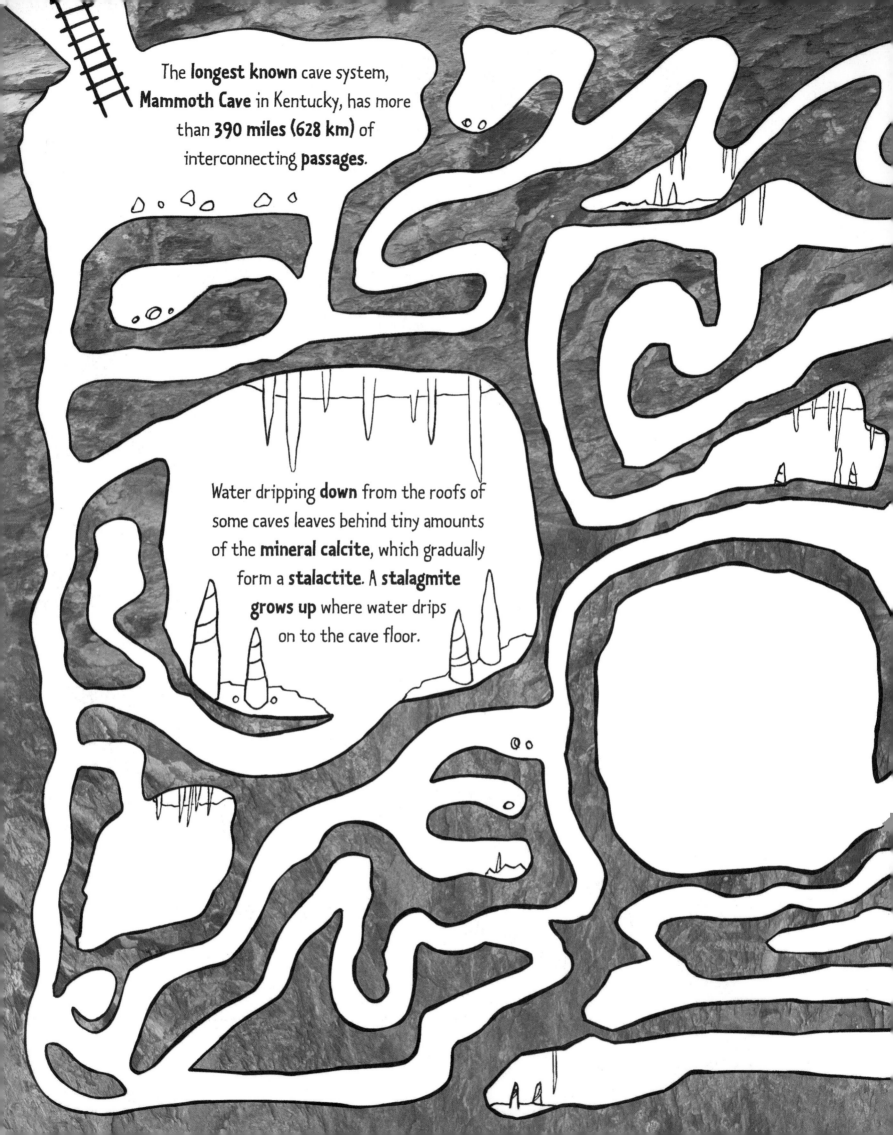

The **longest known** cave system, **Mammoth Cave** in Kentucky, has more than **390 miles (628 km)** of interconnecting **passages**.

Water dripping **down** from the roofs of some caves leaves behind tiny amounts of the **mineral calcite**, which gradually form a **stalactite**. A **stalagmite grows up** where water drips on to the cave floor.

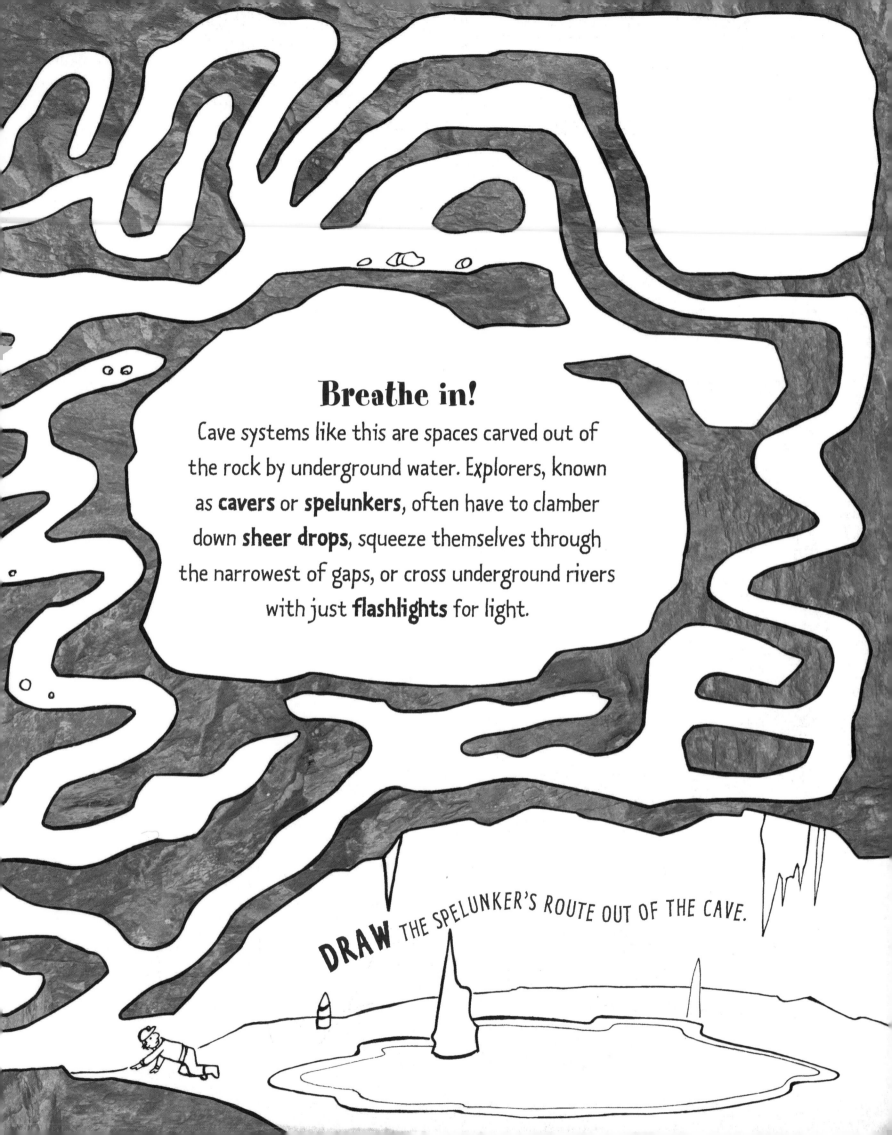

Breathe in!

Cave systems like this are spaces carved out of the rock by underground water. Explorers, known as **cavers** or **spelunkers**, often have to clamber down **sheer drops**, squeeze themselves through the narrowest of gaps, or cross underground rivers with just **flashlights** for light.

DRAW THE SPELUNKER'S ROUTE OUT OF THE CAVE.

In the **future**, there will need to be rules about driving the **sky highways**—you can't paint yellow lines or have median strips up there!

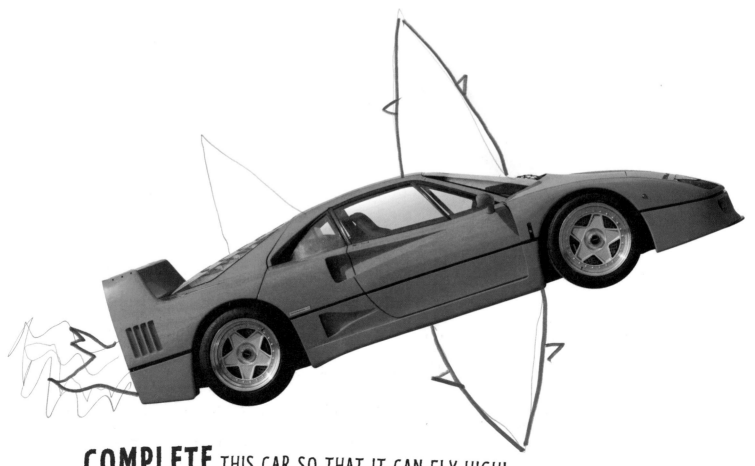

COMPLETE THIS CAR SO THAT IT CAN FLY HIGH!

Curtiss Autoplane 1917

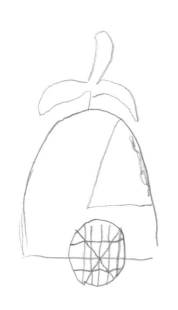

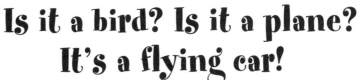

Is it a bird? Is it a plane? It's a flying car!

People have been fascinated by the idea of flying cars for years. The **Curtiss Autoplane**, with its removable wings and tail, was designed in 1917—however, it hopped rather than flew! Some recent designs include the **Moller M400 Skycar**, designed to fly up to 360 mph (579 kph), the gyroplane car **PAL-V**, with speeds of up to 112 mph (180 kph), and the **Terrafugia Transition**, which has fold-away wings and speeds of 105–115 mph (172–185 kph).

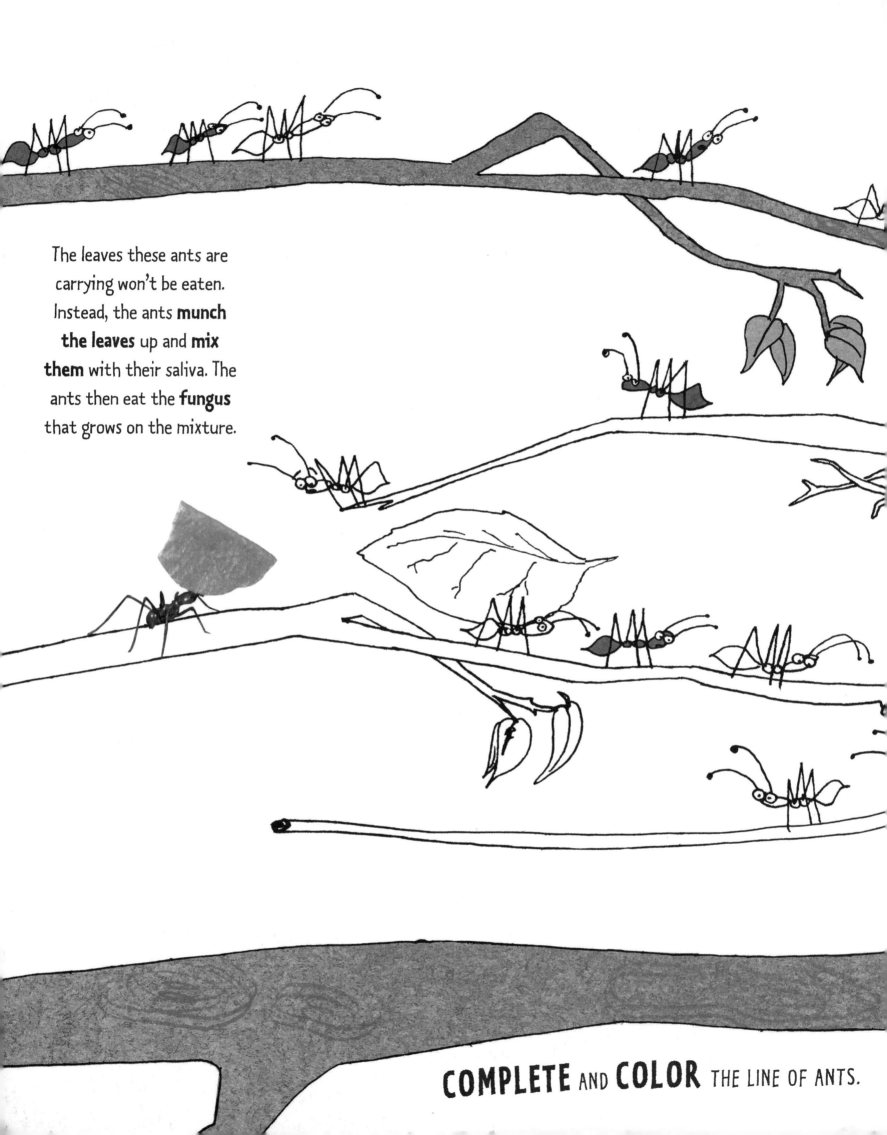

The leaves these ants are carrying won't be eaten. Instead, the ants **munch the leaves** up and **mix them** with their saliva. The ants then eat the **fungus** that grows on the mixture.

COMPLETE AND **COLOR** THE LINE OF ANTS.

As strong as an...ant?

A $\frac{1}{3}$-inch- (1-cm-) long **leaf-cutter ant** can climb 100-ft (30-m) trees, cut off pieces of leaf (which can weigh 50 times its body weight), then, following a special scent trail, **carry** these back to its **underground nest**. Imagine the equivalent for you—it would mean walking several miles with a medium-sized van on your back!

An **ant's nest** can be the size of a **small car**!

Technical sneakers!

Designing **sneakers** is a complicated business. Obviously, they have to look cool, but that's only part of the story. Each style is carefully designed, using the latest materials, for a **specific sport**. Track athletes, for example, use **spikes**—incredibly light shoes with a thin rubber sole, a top made of mesh, and special spikes on the bottom to help them grip the track.

High-top shoes were originally designed for basketball. They came high up, over the ankle to support the joint as the player sprinted and jumped.

Jordan

Mario rocks

DESIGN YOUR OWN SNEAKER PATTERN AND LOGO.

In 2007, Ken Courtney, an American fashion designer, made five pairs of **gold-dipped** high-top basketball shoes. They sold for $4,000 a pair, making them the **world's most expensive** sneakers!

Mario rocks

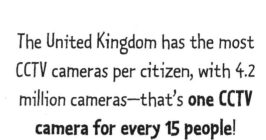

The United Kingdom has the most CCTV cameras per citizen, with 4.2 million cameras—that's **one CCTV camera for every 15 people!**

DRAW WHAT IS HAPPENING ON THE MONITORS.

According to statistics, a person can be caught on camera up to **300 times** a day!

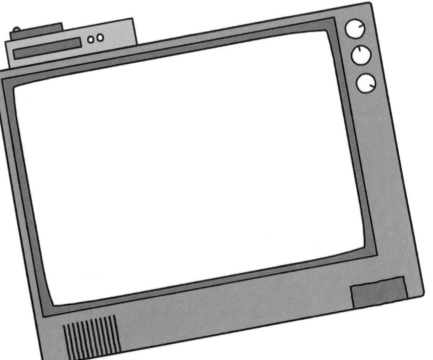

They're watching you!

Video cameras are used around the world to help us watch and observe. These video cameras form a system called **Closed-circuit television (CCTV)**. CCTV cameras are used for different reasons, from **protecting valuables and property**, observing the public, and even in factories to **monitor procedures** that are too dangerous for humans to be near. CCTV is used to **prevent crimes**, but it is also seen as an **invasion** of people's **privacy**.

What's up there?

If you look up into a clear **night sky**, it's amazing how many different things you can see. Using just your eyes or a telescope, you can spot **the Moon**, hundreds of **stars**, and sometimes even a **shooting star**. Look for **planets** such as Venus or Jupiter, too. Planets are much closer to us than the stars, so they look like **small, bright disks** in the sky. You may also see some **slow-moving** specks of light. These are man-made **satellites** that circle our planet.

A **shooting star** is not really a star at all, but a **meteor**. It is a lump of rock or other debris from space that burns up as it enters the Earth's **atmosphere**.

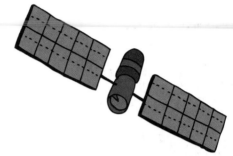

The easiest **satellite** to spot is the **International Space Station**, because it is very big. It completes an **orbit** of the Earth every 90 minutes. It is often mistaken for a **UFO**!

Giant wheels!

Monster trucks are normal **pickup-style trucks** that have been **customized** with **beefed-up engines** and **giant tires**. Monster trucks are powerful so they can drive over obstacles, such as dirt ramps and normal road cars. Monster trucks can be up to 12 ft (3.5 m) high—that's as high as you, with two of your friends standing on your shoulders! With **giant wheels** and lots of crazy stunts, the monster trucks need really big and **powerful suspensions**, but even then it's a bumpy ride!

Monster trucks are customized in lots of different ways, ranging from colorful patterns to sculpted dinosaur designs!

A new set of giant tires can cost around $12,500—that's a lot of allowance money!

DRAW SOMETHING AMAZING TO COMPLETE THE BOOK.

Goodbye!

Shoham's Bangle

To Nana Aziza, Abba Naji, and their children—
who left Baghdad with one small suitcase and a
lot of heart—who taught me that being together
is what matters. And for David, Eliyahu, Shlomo,
Yosef, and Refael, because you are what matter.
—S.S.

To my grandmothers, who immigrated to Israel
from different sides of the world.
—N.K.

Shoham's Bangle

Sarah Sassoon
illustrated by Noa Kelner

KAR-BEN
PUBLISHING

Nana Aziza and I share a jingle-jangle of bangles. She has many. I have one.

Our bangles make clink-clanking music when we chip-chop garlic and onions.

They cut perfectly round date cookies when we bake.

They glitter golden in the sun when we pick figs from our garden.

Best of all, Nana Aziza has taught me that if I don't want to forget something, I can move my bangle from one wrist to the other—my own special golden reminder.

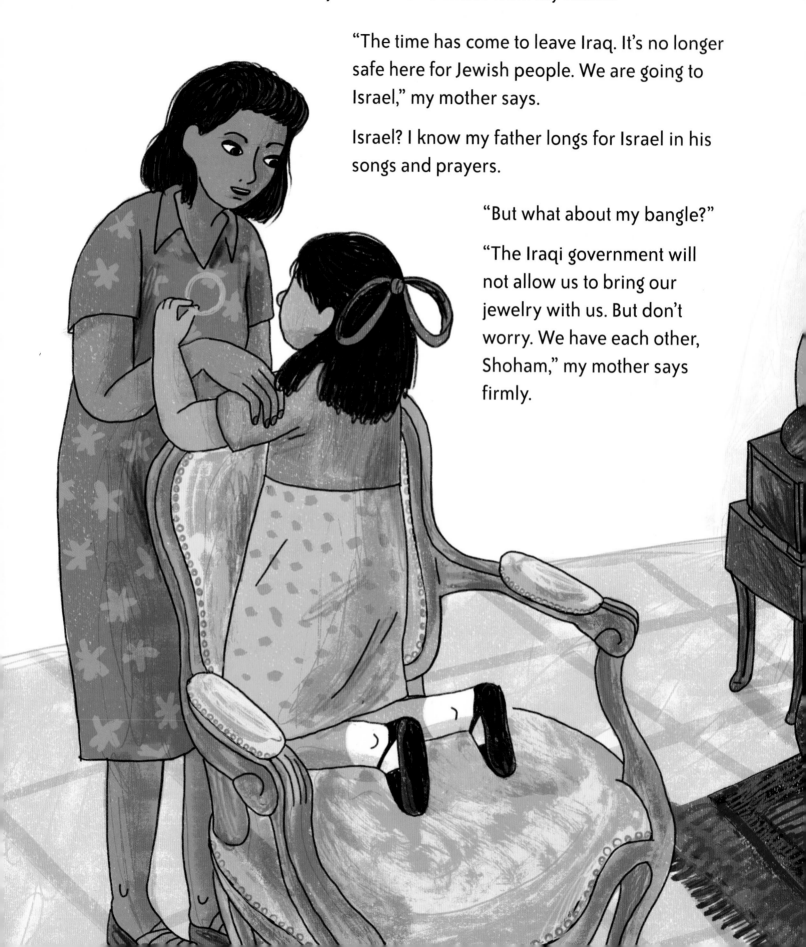

One morning my mother slips my bangle off my wrist, and my whole world slides from my hands.

"The time has come to leave Iraq. It's no longer safe here for Jewish people. We are going to Israel," my mother says.

Israel? I know my father longs for Israel in his songs and prayers.

"But what about my bangle?"

"The Iraqi government will not allow us to bring our jewelry with us. But don't worry. We have each other, Shoham," my mother says firmly.

I don't ask about leaving our house and fig tree.

We are allowed only one suitcase for our whole family: my parents, Nana, myself, and my brothers—M'rad, Baruch, Sabach, and Menashe.

I run to Nana Aziza to check if she knows, to hold her hand, and hear her bangles' music telling me everything will be all right. But Nana is not in her room. She's in the kitchen baking.

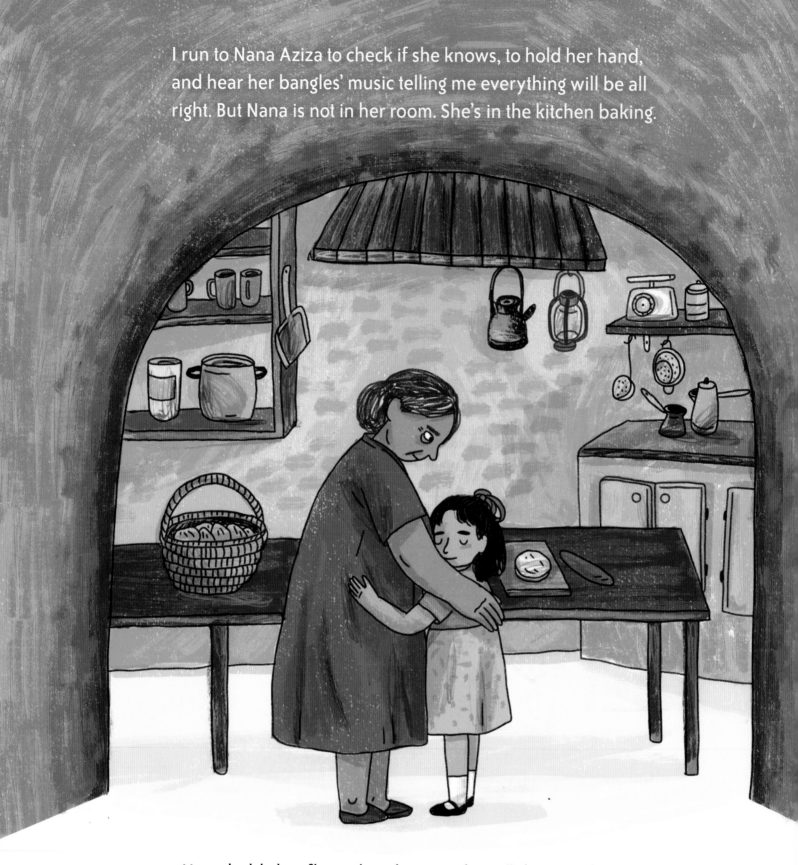

Nana holds her floury hands toward me. "The Jewish people left Egypt with matzah. We will leave Baghdad with pita."

Nana's arms are bare, her bangles gone.

She notices my sad face.

"Don't worry. We have each other, Shoham." And she hands me a blue cloth bag, heavy with pita bread.

"Hold this tight, Shoham. Don't lose it, no matter what."

I hold the bag tight. I need to be brave. I will not let the bag go.

The airport is crowded with families hauling their suitcases. We stand tightly packed, like rolled grape leaves in the hot sun. Men and women in uniforms check all the suitcases. Pockets are emptied out. I cling tightly to my cloth bag.

"Open it," the man at the gate commands.

He puts his hand in. I look up at Nana and hold my breath. What if he takes the pita bread away? What will we eat?

I breathe again when the man gives me back the bag and waves us forward.

I hold on to Nana as we climb the metal stairs. We've never been on an airplane before. It's like climbing onto a giant eagle.

The plane is packed, smelly with sweat, and noisy with cries. I touch my wrist—to twist my bangle and comfort myself—but my wrist is empty. I clutch the bag of pita in one hand and Nana's hand in the other.

The airplane roars down the runway, takes off, and soars into the sky.

"We are going to the land of Israel," my father says, his voice bittersweet like etrog jam. My little brothers cry. Someone sings a song from Psalms.

I join the singing as the white clouds surround us like angels' wings.

When my tummy rumbles, I ask Nana, "Can we eat the pita now?"

Nana Aziza smiles. "Not yet. When we arrive in Israel. It won't be long."

It's dark when we land with a bump.

Our parents lead us down the stairs. When our feet touch the ground,
Nana Aziza lets go of my hand, bends down, and kisses the dusty earth.

We ride in an open truck that shakes my bones, until we reach a camp with metal wires around it. I hold my father's hand.

"Don't worry," he tells me. "We have each other."

There are many people, but we manage to find some empty space to settle down.

"We are camping tonight," Nana Aziza says, her smile bright. "On the sand of Israel. The perfect first night in the Holy Land."

The ground is hard. I sit down close to Nana.

"The Israelites slept on the desert floor when they left Egypt," she says. "And now it's time to eat our pita like they ate their matzah."

Finally!

We pass around the pita. I take a small bite.

"Ouch!"

My teeth hit something hard and metal.

Nana laughs.

Carefully, I bite around and around until I uncover my golden bangle.

Nana takes my hand and slips my bangle onto my wrist.

"To remember where we came from, Shoham."

In our new world, I twist and turn my
bangle, moving it from wrist to wrist . . .

to remember Hebrew words,

for luck when I play five stones,

and to shape round semolina cookies.

And every night, before I fall asleep, I twist my bangle one last time, to remember our home by the Tigris River where my fig tree still grows.

Author's Note

I grew up baking date cookies with my own Nana Aziza. Her bangles jangled as she rolled *b'ab'eb' tamar* dough flat and shared our family's stories. She related her memories of growing up by the Tigris River in Al-'Uzair, home to the tomb of Ezra the Scribe. She described how she met my grandfather and how they married and moved to Baghdad. And she retold the story of Operation Ezra & Nehemiah, when she was airlifted to Israel in 1951, with my grandfather, their five children, and 120,000 other Iraqi Jews.

Today I wear my own special bangle given to me by my Nana, to remember her and the ancient Jewish Babylonian world she left behind. To remind myself that it's not about the homes we leave, but about the homes we rebuild.

The author's grandparents with their five children in Baghdad in 1951

About the Author
Sarah Sassoon is an Australian-born poet and writer of Iraqi-Jewish descent who grew up drinking her grandmother's cardamom tea. One of her favorite places is in the kitchen, cooking up stories for her husband, four boys, and dog. She lives in Jerusalem.

About the Illustrator
Noa Kelner graduated from the Bezalel Academy of Art and Design. She works with book publishers, newspapers, and magazines, and loves to give stories color and form. She is the cofounder and artistic director of the annual Outline–Illustration and Words festival in Jerusalem and also teaches illustration. She lives in Jerusalem with her husband and two children.

KAR-BEN PUBLISHING®
An imprint of Lerner Publishing Group, Inc.
241 First Avenue North
Minneapolis, MN 55401 USA

Website address: www.karben.com

Main body text set in Bailey Sans ITC Std. Typeface provided by International Typeface Corp.

Library of Congress Cataloging-in-Publication Data

Names: Sassoon, Sarah, 1981– author. | Kelner, Noa, illustrator.
Title: Shoham's bangle / Sarah Sassoon ; illustrated by Noa Kelner.
Description: Minneapolis, MN : Kar-Ben Publishing, [2022] | Audience: Ages 5–9. | Audience: Grades 2–3. | Summary: "When Shoham's family emigrates from Iraq to Israel, Nana Aziza gives Shoham a way to remember where she came from"— Provided by publisher.
Identifiers: LCCN 2021044147 (print) | LCCN 2021044148 (ebook) | ISBN 9781728438962 (hardcover) | ISBN 9781728439020 (pbk.) | ISBN 9781728461090 (eb pdf)
Subjects: CYAC: Emigration and immigration—Fiction. | Jews—Israel—Fiction. | Family life—Fiction. | Iraq—Fiction. | Israel—Fiction. | LCGFT: Picture books.
Classification: LCC PZ7.1.S26478 Sh 2022 (print) | LCC PZ7.1.S26478 (ebook) | DDC [E]—dc23

LC record available at https://lccn.loc.gov/2021044147
LC ebook record available at https://lccn.loc.gov/2021044148

Manufactured in China
1-1008986-51437-10/19/2022

0623/B2268/A7